INSIDE THE
MIND
of SALES

INSIDE THE MIND *of* SALES

How to understand the mind and sell anything

Derek Borthwick
Dip.C.Hyp/NLP

Copyright © 2020 Derek Borthwick

All rights reserved.

ISBN 9798664092578

No part of this book or accompanying audio may be reproduced, stored in a retrieval system, or transmitted in any form, or by any means, electronic, mechanical, photocopying, recording or otherwise, without prior permission of the author.

DEDICATION

For Skye, Jamie and Adam.

"Real wisdom is realising that you don't know everything."

Derek Borthwick

ABOUT THE AUTHOR

Derek Borthwick, *BSc. (Hons), Dip.C.Hyp/NLP*, has over thirty years' experience in sales, distribution and marketing and has raised over a billion dollars in assets and has worked with some of the world's largest companies. He has lectured at top Scottish Universities and specialises in advanced communication, persuasion and influence methods. Derek gained a diploma in clinical hypnotherapy and is a certified master practitioner of neurolinguistic programming (NLP).

CONTENTS

About The Author vii

Contents ix

PREFACE 1

PART ONE 5
WHERE THE SECRETS LIE

CHAPTER 1 7
Reframing The Picture

CHAPTER 2 13
The Super Computer

CHAPTER 3 20
Making It Real

CHAPTER 4 41
The Power of Belief

CHAPTER 5 53
Managing Your State

CHAPTER 6 71
Rapport Building

CHAPTER 7 82
Getting People To Like You

CHAPTER 8 94
Different Personalities

PART TWO 101
SUCCESSFUL SALES METHODS

CHAPTER 9 103
    The Truth About Sales

CHAPTER 10 114
    Preparing For Success

CHAPTER 11 128
    The Meet And Greet

CHAPTER 12 133
    Asking The Right Questions

CHAPTER 13 144
    Detectives And Funnels

CHAPTER 14 154
    It's Time To Present

CHAPTER 15 175
    Non Verbal Cues

CHAPTER 16 182
    Closing The Sale

CHAPTER 17 205
    Post Sales Meeting

CHAPTER 18 205
    Conclusion

Bonus Rapid Learning Accelerator Audio & Bonus Chapter on Page 206

PREFACE

"If you want to become a great communicator, then become more aware."

This is the book that I've always wanted to write. During my career of over 30 years in sales, I have attended numerous training courses, read many books and have learnt a great deal.

However, for me, there was always something missing. The missing pieces in the jigsaw puzzle. I was determined to find those pieces and to see the full picture. This study led me to look at the scientific principles behind persuasion and influence. On my journey, I have studied hypnosis and neurolinguistic programming (NLP) which can best be described as software for the mind. This has led to a much deeper understanding of how humans communicate, think, and process the world.

In this book, I'm going to share with you the secrets that I have discovered, together with the things that have worked for me. From the moment that I started my career in sales, I have been fascinated why some people are successful, and others struggle. This led to a fascination with human behaviour and a curiosity as to what motivates people and why they behave in the way that they do? My quest led me to discover that the secret

PREFACE

to successful selling lies way beyond basic sales techniques and processes, and comes from combining different disciplines.

On my journey, I discovered I did many things naturally. However, there were things that I had missed and was not aware of. During this journey, I discovered that the vast majority of what we do takes place at an unconscious level. I discovered many of the secrets over time and I thought that others had too. However, it was not until speaking with others that it became apparent that this was not the case. It was at this point that I realised the need to share this.

Most of the training that I had received previously focused on conscious learning processes. However, there is so much more going on outwith our awareness that governs our decisions, choices and behaviours. This led me to an in-depth study of how our brains, minds, and nervous systems work. As part of the research, I discovered that to be successful in sales requires an understanding of advanced communication and sharpened awareness skills.

My journey first began when I came across hypnosis back in the mid-1980s. A stage hypnotist came to the University of Sheffield where I was studying at the time. I was intrigued and bought tickets along with my fellow students. At the show, I was fascinated and it was then that I realised the power of the mind. How could one individual make other people do these unusual things? As soon as the show finished, I promptly ran over to the hypnotist and asked him how he did those things. I got little of an answer, I'm afraid. However, that fascination stayed with me and has drawn me to research how and why this worked and what we can learn from this.

PREFACE

My research took me into the world of clinical hypnosis, stage hypnosis, neurolinguistic programming (NLP), neuroscience, and into the world of persuasion and influence. Combining these disciplines, together with traditional sales approaches and my own extensive experience, allowed me to develop something very special. These methods and processes are very powerful and work. They literally will transform the way that you approach sales. Following the principles in this book will ensure your success not only in sales, but across your personal, family, and intimate relationships.

I truly believe that this is the complete sales approach and may just be the only book that you will ever need.

How to Use This Book

This book is divided into 2 parts.

Part One

Part one covers how the brain, nervous system, and mind work. This is the real secret to being successful in sales and any form of communication. This is the part where all the secrets lie. It is important to return to this part as needed.

Part Two

Part two gives a step by step structured approach to sales. This gives you a framework and steps to follow, and when combined with the information in stage one, gives the complete package of how to master sales and communication.

PREFACE

Free Bonus

Included is a bonus Rapid Learning Accelerator Program. "Program Your Mind for Success" is an audio track that is available free (See Page 206). It is recommended to use earphones when listening to the track. The best time to use this recording is before going to sleep at night, or during a quiet period during the day with earphones when you will not be disturbed.

Do not use this track when driving, operating any machinery or when you need to be alert.

The Sum of the Total Is Greater Than the Sum of the Parts

Combining these three parts will provide you with a very powerful, effective and easy method to become persuasive, influential and successful across all your sales and communication skills.

The Journey Is Not the Trip

There is a lot of information in this book, and it is best to view this as an ongoing development plan, where you can refine your skills as you go along. Make sure that you read the first part of the book carefully before moving to the second part and remember to use the audio download daily for at least 30 days. The principles discussed in this book will massively improve your communication skills across the range of your business, personal, family, and intimate communications.

I'm excited to begin, so let's get started.

PART ONE

Where The Secrets Lie

IMPORTANT

Download your Bonus Rapid Learning Accelerator Audio now & Bonus Chapter "The Hot Button."

You will find the details of how to download these at the end of Chapter 18

CHAPTER 1

Reframing The Picture

"If you don't like the picture, change the frame."

Let's be honest, when people hear the word "sales" it sometimes conjures up a negative image. It is often an activity that we have to do, and that many of us don't want to. Often, we imagine people who are manipulative, pushy, and we perceive them as trying to sell us something that we don't want. We may have had an unpleasant experience that has coloured our view and yet it can be one of the most rewarding and satisfying careers to engage in, as long as it is done properly.

CHANGING THE FRAME

Before beginning, let's define sales.

Merriam Webster Dictionary

"Operations and activities involved in promoting and selling goods or services"

"One who sells in a given territory, in a store, or by telephone."

My Definition of Sales

"The communication of an idea, product, or service, from one person to another that causes them to take action that will result in either removing pain, solving a problem or enhancing their life."

Many people say that they are not involved in sales and that there isn't a need to learn any sales skills. Others say that it's not relevant to them. If you are trying to persuade somebody around to your point of view in an argument, you are involved in sales. If you are trying to get your children to bed on time, you're involved in sales. If you want to get others to go to a restaurant or holiday destination of your choice, then you're involved in sales.

Every job is in some way related to sales. It is the lifeblood of any company and without it, there would be no new business to enable a company to grow.

Language is Powerful.

Think about the words "campaigner" and "protester." They have very different connotations and can be applied in many cases to the same thing. I think of sales as an advanced form of communication, with an intense desire to understand and to help a customer or client solve a problem or achieve a desired outcome. Salespeople often have to go out and visit customers or speak to them on the phone, and many don't enjoy doing so. Let's see how we can reframe this.

"If You Don't Like the Picture Change the Frame"

Think about a glass that contains fifty per cent of water. We can describe the glass as being half empty or half full. Both statements are factually correct and are just different ways of looking at the same thing. Consider a picture with a frame around it. When the frame is changed around that picture, it looks different. This is called reframing. It is the same scenario, just looked at differently. The picture should look the same, but the contrast is different, and this affects how the picture looks.

Let's look at how we can view sales in a new way. If you are a salesperson, then you are being paid by your company to go out and to learn, gain, and practice communication skills. These are skills that are not only going to benefit your work but your family and personal life as well. If you had to finance this yourself, it would be expensive.

Once you reframe what it is you do, it takes on a different perspective. Remember, you can choose the frame. Either the glass is half empty or half full, you decide. Reframing is a very important part of the sales process. To quote Thomas Edison, inventor of the electric lightbulb,

> *"I have not failed. I've just found 10,000 ways that won't work."*

LEARNING TO LEARN

Sharpening Up

If you want to be a better salesperson, sharpen your awareness. This is true not just in sales, but in all walks of life. Add to this a robust and repeatable process, and all the ingredients for success are in place. New skills are best learnt through practice and in small bite-sized chunks.

Learning to Learn

We have two minds, the conscious and the unconscious mind. Sometimes the unconscious mind is referred to as the subconscious mind. Let's look at the two minds in more detail.

The Conscious Mind

The conscious mind is the rational, analytical, and critical part of the mind. It controls "willpower" and short term memory together with analysing our internal thoughts. It also runs an internal check on the information that is coming in and compares this with what we believe to be true. If the information matches what we believe to be true, the belief is reinforced. If the information contradicts what is believed, then the new suggestion is rejected, and no change in behaviour or beliefs occurs.

The Unconscious Mind

The unconscious mind is far more powerful than the conscious mind. However, it has limited ability to make judgments, and it relies on the critical factor within the conscious mind to do this. It is the emotional mind, and it controls our habits, behaviours and its job is to keep us safe. The unconscious mind also regulates breathing, blood pressure, heartbeat, together with many other unconscious processes. The unconscious mind is over a million times more powerful than the conscious mind.

Think of the conscious mind as the driver of the bus and the unconscious mind as the bus.

The Four Stages of Learning

When learning a new skill, we go through four stages of learning and these are listed below.

1. Unconscious Incompetence. We are unaware that we don't know how to do something.

2. Conscious Incompetence. We are aware that we don't know how to do something.

3. Conscious Competence. We can now do something but must concentrate, and it is not yet natural.

4. Unconscious Competence. The skill is now hard-wired and we can do it without thinking.

Learning from Chicken Sexers

Separating the egg producing female from male chicks has important commercial value and is a skill called "sexing." The best chicken sexers come from Japan. Separating males from females is difficult, as both look identical to the untrained eye. The training method involves training the brain through trial and error until it becomes an unconscious process. Something that can seem impossible to begin with soon becomes an unconscious, competent process.

When learning a new skill, it is important to realise the four stages of learning. When going through this book, there may be things that you may be aware of and do well, and there will be things that you are not aware of. The key is to break things down and practice them. Trying to learn everything all at once can cause a feeling of being overwhelmed. Work through the book, paying particular attention to state control and rapport, and practice as often as possible and in as many environments as you can.

CHAPTER 2

The Super Computer

"We should take care not to make the intellect our god; it has, of course, powerful muscles, but no personality."

Albert Einstein

Most people think that they have one brain. We actually have three "brains", each performing specialised functions. This three brain model became known as the "triune model" from the work of Paul MacLean. While there have been further refinements, it serves as a good metaphor.

THE THREE BRAINS

The three brains are:
1. Reptilian, Stem Brain or Paleocortex.
2. Mammalian, Midbrain, or Limbic System.
3. Human or Neocortex brain.

Understanding the Triune

The reptilian or paleocortex filters all the incoming messages and handles most of the fight, flight or freeze responses. It is also responsible for some of the very basic and strong primitive emotions. Its primary responsibility is not with thinking, but with survival. When driving a car, if somebody suddenly jumps out in front of the car, we don't want to think about applying the brakes. It's done automatically for us by the reptilian brain. The reptilian brain does not process details well, it only passes along big obvious chunks of concrete data.

The midbrain, also known as the mammalian brain or the limbic system, is sometimes referred to as the chimp brain. It makes sense of social situations, attaches meaning to situations and is the emotional centre.

The neocortex is the outer part of the brain responsible for critical thinking, logic, and analyses any sales proposition. However, the information has to pass through the reptilian brain, to the midbrain and on to the neocortex, to be analysed and critiqued.

Spotting a Pirate

Our brain makes its best guestimate of reality based on the data entering it and is constantly refining the model. If reality is as predicted, then the information is processed largely at an unconscious level. If something unexpected happens in the environment, this may be raised to consciousness to be processed, assessed, and evaluated.

Let's imagine walking down the street on our way to work on a Monday morning. As we walk down the street suddenly, we see a man dressed as a pirate. This would be unusual and would not be expected or predicted. Immediately, this is raised to consciousness. The brain has to make sense of this new information. Our reptilian survival brain kicks in and decides if the pirate is a friend or foe. Next, the mammalian or limbic system puts context around the experience and produces an emotion. It may be laughter, curiosity, or anger.

Finally, the information is passed to the neocortex. This is the moment that we have all had after witnessing something unusual when we try to make sense of it. We often speak to ourselves and say, "Why would somebody be dressed like a pirate in the middle of Edinburgh on a Monday morning?"

Understanding the Reptile

The reptilian brain works, based on:

- Is something a threat or a danger?
- Is something new and exciting?
- If it is new, get to the point quickly and make it simple.
- If it is not new and unexpected, then ignore it.

What Does This Mean for the Sales Experience?

- If you are boring, you will be ignored.
- If you are a threat, you will be ignored.
- If something is complicated, it will be ignored.

What to Do

- Pique another person's interest.
- Avoid being seen as a threat, intellectually or socially.

- Make things simple to understand.
- Build rapport rapidly.

Working With the Reptile and the Chimp

When first meeting somebody, the brain is assessing whether they are a friend or foe. It then tries to reference the experience and an emotional response is generated as it tries to provide some context. Finally, we critically evaluate the information to make sense of it and to formulate our opinion.

Yet, think about what happens in a typical business situation. First, we try to appeal to the critical brain and try to "logic" somebody into a decision. Then we hope that the customer feels good about us. Finally, we hope that they have not perceived us as a threat. This approach is the inverse to how our brains work.

Let's use an example to illustrate this. Suppose that you are looking for a partner to form an intimate relationship with. Let's assume that you are in a bar or a nightclub and you see somebody that you like. Imagine walking up to that person and presenting them with a list of ten reasons to go out with you on a date. Having presented the list to them, you then start to explain logically why they should go out with you. How successful would this approach be? Exactly, although bizarrely enough in the odd case, the approach might work as a pattern interrupt. More of this later. In most cases, people would just think of this as unusual behaviour and yet, is this not what we do in business?

The Super Computer

Learning to Trade

When presenting something, we must make sure that the reptilian brain is interested and not threatened or confused. This short story illustrates how important it is to make sure that the people that you are presenting to don't feel threatened but follow and understand exactly what you are saying.

I saw an advert for a free training session showing how to trade in currency to be held at one of the local hotels. With my background in Investment Management, I decided to attend the event to find out a bit more about currency trading and to see how the event was being run.

I arrived at the hotel, parked my car outside, and entered the main room, where there were about twenty people seated. The presentation started, and we were shown an introductory video. The video was professionally shot and showed the expertise and credibility of the company, together with the currency trading system.

After the video had finished, the presenter, a well-educated man in his early thirties, explained that he was going to demystify currency trading and was going to demonstrate a live trade during the presentation. I realised that there would be a sales pitch and upsell at the end, but I was curious to see how the pitch was going to be presented. He began by making things very simple and explained some basics of currency trading. Then, as things progressed, it gradually became a bit more technical. At one point, he used a graph to illustrate a point, but my attention momentarily had wandered. The point was critical to understanding the trading strategy, and I felt slightly uneasy, as I was now not following what he was saying. I could feel the frustration building. To reduce frustration and seek clarity, I did what many of us would do. I put my hand up to ask a question. My reptilian brain had kicked in. I was confused.

Then something bizarre happened. The presenter dismissively, while pointing at me with the back of his hand, stated that he was not taking questions. I had driven to the venue, spent money on parking and I thought it perfectly reasonable to be want to understand the presentation. I now could not follow what was going on and was beginning to feel even more uneasy. I raised my hand again. The presenter then rather rudely said, *"Look, I'm not taking questions!"* and I said to him, *"Well, if you are not going to take any questions, how am I supposed to follow what you are talking about?"* He then repeated, *"I am not taking questions!"*

Confusion had now turned to annoyance. I was now acting from my reptile and midbrain and did something completely illogical. After being in the presentation for only ten minutes, I closed my book and got up and left with the internal voice in my head saying, *"I'm not listening to another word of this, this is complete nonsense!"*

On arrival back home and having had time to reflect and critically evaluate what had happened, I realised that leaving early was not the wisest thing to have done. I had missed out on both learning the information and the formula for the event. My reptile brain had kicked in and together with it, my midbrain. My critical brain had not had the chance to analyse whether my actions were logical. The reptile brain had caused a shutdown in my critical thinking and created the fight or flight response. I simply had to leave the room. This story just goes to show you how we can all act irrationally, and even though I understand how the brain works, I was still at its mercy.

If we put this in the context of a sales presentation, if you are going to confuse your customers, and not treat them with respect, then you are likely to experience a shut down in their thinking. This is before they even get to evaluate your proposition. The confused mind always says no and the suspicious mind always says no. In this particular story, the confused mind said *"No"*, and *"let's get out of here!"*

CHAPTER 3

Making It Real

"The only true wisdom is in knowing you know nothing."

Socrates

Much of sales training focuses on techniques and procedures. While it is useful to understand these, the real secret lies with an understanding of how people perceive the world and what their map of the world looks like. There are four magic ingredients that we need to be aware of when communicating.

FOUR MAGIC INGREDIENTS

The four magic ingredients are belief, state control, rapport, and a sharpened awareness (BSRA). These are skills that you can take with you and use not just in a sales environment but in any business, personal or intimate setting.

    I have witnessed people who were not technically good or structured in the sales process and yet have been very successful. In the past, they were often described as "characters." They unconsciously understood many aspects of belief, state control, rapport, and awareness (BSRA).

I've also seen people who were very structured and followed everything in a step-by-step manner but who were unsuccessful. They lacked external awareness and were unaware of belief, state control, rapport, and awareness (BSRA). Before we explore these ingredients, let's explore how we create reality. What is reality and is reality the same for everyone?

WHAT IS REALITY?

Some may wonder why there is a focus on reality in a sales book. This may seem a bit philosophical. However, for us to be successful and to be great communicators, we must have a good grasp on what this is and the findings may surprise you.

Is It Real or Not?

For many, the sound of fingernails being dragged over a blackboard is unpleasant. For others, they dislike the sound of hands being rubbed against an inflated balloon. For people who dislike either of these, simply vividly imagining the experience can cause real discomfort. The better the imagination is engaged in the experience, then the more profound the effect will be. FMRI scanning of the brain shows that the same parts of the brain are activated when something is vividly imagined and when actually experienced. This may seem a difficult concept to accept, and to illustrate this, we must enter the world of hypnosis.

An exploration of hypnosis shows that reality can be hijacked and overridden. The mind can be accessed under hypnosis, so much so that if a coin is placed on the skin, a blister can develop on removal if a posthypnotic suggestion is given to that effect. Dave Elman is one of the father figures of hypnosis. Elman trained medical professionals and dentists in using hypnosis for medical procedures. Elman would ask the dentists in his training classes to come forward, one after another, to be hypnotised. While under hypnosis, another dentist would probe the gingival, very sensitive, area of the mouth with a sharp dental probe. The dentist under hypnosis would feel no pain.

The Big Filter

We create our reality by filtering the data that comes in through the primary senses. The brain makes its best interpretation of this data and with it a guesstimate of reality. Yes, that is correct. We are not seeing what is out there but rather the brain's best guesstimate of what is there.

This is a hard concept for many to accept. However, as we go through this section, I will show you how you can satisfy this for yourself. The brain constructs reality not by what we are seeing, hearing or feeling but by what it expects to see, hear and feel. These expectations are based on all its prior experiences and memories. The model is constructed and based on what has worked in the past.

If the brain's predicted reality is disrupted, it may take more time to process the data or more attention may be given to this unpredicted reality. If everything goes along with no unexpected surprises the visual system will miss much of what's going on around us. Think of driving home. You probably remember little about the journey home unless something unusual occurs. If while driving home a lion darted across the road, this would be an unexpected, unpredicted event and would be raised to awareness for processing. The incident would be remembered. The lion would be a pattern interrupt. This can explain how something can be controversial or outrageous to begin with and, through repetition, becomes accepted as the norm and, in many cases, not even noticed. The novelty factor quickly fades.

70s Punk Rock

Back in the 1970s, in the UK, punk rock erupted onto the scene and with it a whole new style of dressing and body piercing. At the time, it was regarded as outrageous for a man to wear an earring and to have a bright coloured Mohican hairstyle. In current times we probably wouldn't even notice and yet at that time, judgements were made. If we look back to when The Beatles and The Rolling Stones first came upon the scene, they had long hair. Yet if we look in today's environment, we wouldn't even notice that type of hairstyle. Interestingly, many of yesterday's rebels are now part of today's establishment and many have been knighted for their endeavours. Being original only lasts for so long. Now have a look at the following text.

**OUR BRAINS
CAN BE A
A MYSTERY**

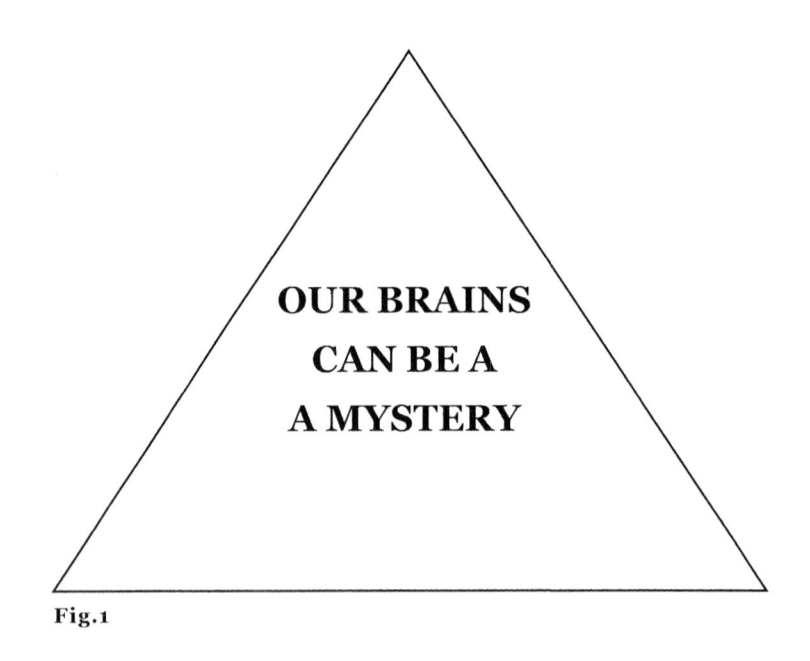

Fig.1

How Could You Miss It?

Did you read "our brains can be a mystery?" Are you sure? Read it again word by word. Most people miss the two "A"s. We don't spot everything. The brain makes its model of reality based on its best guesstimate. When things are out of context, then that is when they become the most noticeable. I am sure we have all had a situation when we didn't notice anything new.

I remember working in an office. I arrived one day and upon entering the office, one of my colleagues asked me what I thought of the new sign. I replied, "What new sign?" They then greeted me with a look of sheer disbelief that I had not seen it. With knowledge of how the brain works, it makes sense why I had not seen the sign. We don't see with our eyes; we see with our brains. I did not see the sign because my brain did not expect to see it. The sign was at the side of the main door and was out of my foveal or focused vision. Without prior knowledge that the sign had been erected, my brain did not expect to see it. Its best guesstimate of reality did not include the new sign. It ignored any sensory data to that effect. This has important implications for the sales process, which we will return to later.

Have you ever wandered around the house looking for something and not been able to find it? I have often done this when looking for my keys. Then the moment it is pointed out that they are right in front of my eyes, they come into vision. Hypnotists call this a negative hallucination and it is a sign of deep trance!

Predictive Machines

Human beings are predictive machines that are constantly refining our model of the world based on predictions. We think that we are aware of our surroundings, but we may be blocking out over ninety five per cent of what is happening. Magicians are aware of this and use this to their advantage. This is a tough concept for many to grasp.

Our eyes only give us part of what we see. The rest is done by our brains in stages. Photoreceptors in our eyes convert light into electrochemical data signals. The data coming in is then passed through the optic nerve and converted into electrochemical stimuli as patterns. The brain then interprets these patterns of data to make sense of them and to build up a representation.

Getting Cross

Each human eye has the resolution of roughly a megapixel camera. How then do we get such a high resolution picture of the world? The answer to that is the brain uses its predictive powers and fills in the blanks. If not convinced by this, simply try this brief experiment. When it is safe to do so, pick a point straight ahead of you. Nod your head up and down. Notice what happens to the image. It doesn't move that much and is fairly static. Now take your camera out and hold it in front of you as you watch the screen. Pivot your camera up and down similarly to how you rocked your head. Now, what has happened to the image? It moves around a lot, doesn't it? That's why when you take a video inside any vehicle that is bumping around or view some video footage when running, it bumps around all over the place, just like a TV reporter on the run. Still not convinced?

Let's look at a little exercise that can show you how your brain fills in the gaps based on what it thinks should be there. The human eye contains rods and cones, which are photoreceptors. There is a blind spot in the back of the eye where the optic nerve connects to the eye and there are no photoreceptors. Any light that lands in this area should not show an image. Take a white piece of paper. Draw a small cross of about one cm or just under half an inch in the centre of the paper. Close one eye and hold the paper in front of you at arm's length. Look straight ahead and move the paper from side to side without allowing your eyes to follow the cross. Keep looking ahead. As you move the paper from side to side very slowly, you will notice that the cross disappears. This is the point of the optic nerve and there is no black spot. The brain fills in the gap based on what it thinks should be there and uses the surrounding white colour as its prediction.

Compare and Contrast

We use contrast to make sense of things. The moon rising on the horizon can look enormous. This is an optical illusion. As it rises higher in the sky, it starts to look smaller. The reason for this is that there are often trees or mountains on the horizon that give some contrast. This artificially makes the moon look bigger. We know that colours can appear differently depending on the surrounding colour, and cosmetic companies use this contrast principle to enhance beauty.

Have a look at this picture below. Which circle in the centre is larger, the one on the left, or the one on the right?

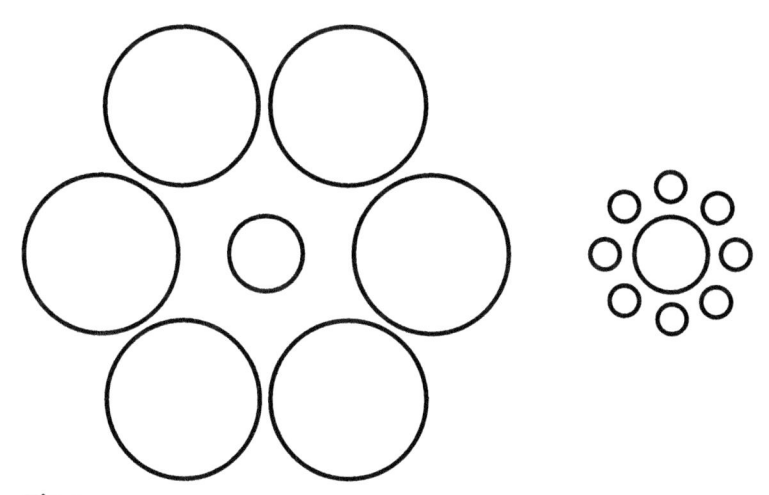

Fig.2

Would it surprise you to learn that both central circles are the same size? Try measuring them.

The sheer amount of data coming into the brain is too much to process consciously. We are constantly being bombarded by external data and yet we are only aware of a tiny part of it. Not convinced? You are now aware of the feelings in your left foot, the temperature in the room, and any background noise. You are now aware of any clothing that may be touching your skin. All the sensory data was already coming in through your senses, but was just not being raised to consciousness.

The brain doesn't cope very well with no sensory input coming in. Solitary confinement in darkness has been used as a punishment and with no sensory input to process, hallucinations take place. The brain cannot deal with no sensory input and is constantly making up its reality and with it our map of the world.

MAKING MAPS

Reality is therefore only ever the brain's best guesstimate and each one of us will interpret reality differently. This is done as a type of map. These maps are based on an interpretation of sensory data, rather than the way things are. This explains why we like different things such as food, music, sport and are attracted to different partners. It also explains why one person can look and see the beauty in something, while it is missed on another.

The data that the brain receives has been filtered, distorted, deleted, and generalised to form a map that is unique to every one of us. Another way to think about this is to imagine that your brain is like a television antenna. Television programs are being broadcast in the form of waves. These waves are picked up by

Making it Real

the television antenna and converted into images by the television. Even two different television sets tuned to the same channel will have slightly different pictures based on the decoding method within the television.

Human beings are all tuned to different channels and these are changing. Imagine that two news programs are broadcasting the news. Both cover similar events but with a different perspective. If you are watching one channel and I am watching another, both programs will have different perspectives on the events of the day. Each will choose what to report on, and what not to report on. This interpretation of the news represents a generalisation, distortion, and deletion that occurs in our brains all the time. We are not seeing what actually happened from the events of the day. We are seeing an interpretation of the events of the day.

Have a look at the next image. What do you see? A vase or two faces?

Fig.3

Our Two Maps of Reality

There are two maps of reality. People are familiar with the external reality, which is perceived through the external senses in the here and now. However, there is an internal map of reality as well. This is based on previous memories and experiences that have already been coded via our five senses. It is possible to be in the here and now and also flip internally to imagine or recall something.

Many people are not aware of these two maps. There is an external awareness, but very few consider the internal map. Within this internal map, our memory is accessed by recalling pictures, sounds, touch, tastes, smells, emotions, and talking to ourselves. If I was to ask about the best holiday or vacation that you had ever been on, you would have to access the memory associated with that event and then describe the experience. The way each one of us recalls events is different and peculiar to each one of us.

Visual Recall

If I was to ask you to recall your favourite holiday or vacation, most of the recall would be done unconsciously. For some of us, we may imagine a picture of being on holiday. However, if asking people to describe the memory further by asking questions like, is it a picture, or is it moving like a movie? Is it in colour, or is it black and white? Is the picture blurry or is it sharply in focus? What size is the picture? For some, they would have to think very hard about this, as it is not normally in conscious awareness. All these different variables represent coding or submodalities of how the memory is stored.

Try this for yourself. Recall an event that was significant and very pleasurable for you. How big is it? Where is it? Draw a frame around it. Is it still or moving? Is it black and white or is it in colour? Is it in focus or is it blurred? Are you seeing the memory through your own eyes or are you watching it a bit like being at a movie theatre? Pay attention to the image that appears. It is possible to change the components of the memory to affect how the memory is experienced. Being aware that this is even taking place is a major step towards being more aware.

Feeling Recall

Many people recall a memory by recalling a feeling. This is a feeling that brings back the experience of that memory. This is difficult to explain to people. Some may just describe it as a summer feeling, for example, or a feeling that they had as a child.

Auditory Recall

Some people recall a particular sound associated with a memory. If recalling a holiday in a beach setting, the trigger for recall may be hearing the sounds associated with that particular memory. We may even hear somebody's voice.

Tasting the Memory

Tastes can be triggers. Some access memories through smell and taste triggers. When I was younger, I went to the beautiful country of Norway on holiday. The Norwegians have this fabulous ice cream called "Softis", literally soft ice cream. While on holiday, we were treated to Softis by my Norwegian relatives.

Recently when I was in Oslo in Norway, I spotted the sign for Softis and made my way straight to the shop and bought one. As soon as I started eating the ice cream, the memories of when I was younger in Norway came flooding back.

It Sure Smells Good

Smells can be important triggers of memory. Have you ever smelled a fragrance and immediately were reminded of someone?

One of my earliest memories is of being on holiday with my family in Millport on the Isle of Cumbrae in Scotland as a small child. I recall one morning going with my Dad to the baker's shop to get the morning rolls. As we approached the shop, I remember the wonderful smell of baking wafting from the shop. Even years later, when I go into a baker's shop, the smell of fresh bread being baked takes me straight back to that early childhood memory.

Another memory associated with smell relates to when I was staying in Norway with my Gran. My aunt and uncle lived nearby in a newer apartment. As children, we would visit my aunt and uncle and it was a big adventure climbing up the stairs to visit them. On entering the building, there was a smell of newly constructed cement. Now, whenever I enter a building that has just been newly constructed, that smell of cement takes me straight back to that childhood memory.

The Codes for Our Reality

We code our version of reality through our senses in the form of representational systems.

The representational systems are:

Visual - Images

Auditory - Sounds

Auditory Digital - Talking to ourself

Kinaesthetic - Feelings

Olfactory - Smell

Gustatory - Taste

While we use all of these representational systems at different times, most of us have a preferred or dominant system which is known as the "lead representational system." This is not a conscious choice; it takes place at an unconscious level. It has been suggested that the breakdown in representational systems as an approximate are as follows:

Visual - 40% of the population

Kinaesthetic - 40% of the population

Auditory - 20% of the population.

Gustatory and Olfactory represent a low percentage.

Whether or not it is exactly a 40/40/20 split is not important. It is true enough to be true. The main two lead systems that I have found the most useful to identify are visual and kinaesthetic. Therefore, we need to sharpen our awareness to establish this. The big challenge is that we are fighting against our limited attention capabilities.

THE LIMITS OF OUR ATTENTION

George Miller, a cognitive psychologist, published a paper in 1956. It is often interpreted and used to argue the case that the human mind can hold 7 plus or minus 2 pieces of information in conscious awareness. The 7 plus or minus 2 model serves as a good metaphor, but it is more complicated than this. The brain organises information in chunks. Think about your telephone number. How do you remember it? If someone asks for your telephone number, you will have a pattern and grouping of numbers that you use to remember and relay your number.

Let's suppose your telephone number is 0131 234 5678. The grouping of numbers here is 4 3 4. Now try relaying your number in a different grouping of numbers and notice how difficult it is.

If repeated back in a different grouping of numbers, it can sometimes be confusing. This shows how the brain organises information into groups or chunks. We have a limit as to how much information we can process consciously before getting confused. Hypnotists, magicians and pickpockets are aware of this, and use this to their advantage.

IDENTIFYING THE REPRESENTATIONAL SYSTEMS

Let's return to the main preferred representational systems, visual, auditory, and kinaesthetic. A method to identify the type of representational system or lead system is to listen to the types of words used. These words occur in patterns or groups of words. Some examples are as follows:

Visual
- I *see* what you mean.
- This *looks clear* to me.
- I can't seem to *picture* it.

Auditory
- That *sounds* right to me.
- I *hear* what you're saying.
- That *rings* a bell.

Kinaesthetic
- I've got a *handle* on this.
- I'm just not *grasping* the situation.
- I have a good *feeling* about this.

People may say that they are a visual or a kinesthetic person. However, it's not as simple as this. We use all of these representational systems, but people tend to have a preference for one.

For example, an individual may say that they are a kinaesthetic person (emphasis on emotions and feelings) and that they can't create internal images (visual). If this happens, simply ask them how do they remember where they parked their car? This is often accompanied by a look of confusion as the individual realises that they can, and do, construct mental pictures, as they begin to recall where their car is parked. Some people do, however, find it easier to create pictures than others.

Limited Awareness

Trying to work out somebody's preferred or lead representational system based on language is very difficult to master and can only be done with a lot of practice. Our limited capacity for awareness (7 plus or minus 2 pieces of information) or limited bandwidth means that if focusing on analysing language patterns, then this comes at the expense of something else.

I like to think of the brain as a computer. When using your computer, the more programs that are running, the slower the computer will run. The more the brain is overloaded, the harder it becomes to observe things until eventually, it crashes. Hypnotists and pickpockets exploit this limited brain bandwidth by using overload and confusion techniques that distract attention.

Listening

When we are trying to establish which system is the preferred or lead representational system, we can listen to the words that someone uses. The challenge with this is that because of our limited awareness, it just becomes too difficult. For most people, unless they are trained, it requires a lot of practice and takes up a lot of brain bandwidth. It would be useful to have a method whereby it is possible to identify which is somebody's likely preferred representational system, without it requiring too much concentration. Having limited brain bandwidth to interpret things means that we have to make sure that we use it efficiently.

Echo Technique

The most important words that a person hears are the words that they have just said. A very powerful way to build rapport is the "Echo Technique." This technique involves repeating back what the client or customer has just said. At this point, you may say, "I can't do this, people will notice." On the contrary, they will not, and even if they did, you are just clarifying your understanding. Is there anything wrong with that?

Let's have a look at an example.

"I FEEL that it's time to upgrade our IT system as it's a little outdated?"

"So, you FEEL that it's time to upgrade your IT system as it's a little outdated?"

"Yes"

This is then followed by asking about the implications of having an outdated IT system.

"What does it mean for your business to have an outdated IT system?"

"It means that we don't have the flexibility or ability to integrate new processes."

"So you don't have the flexibility or ability to integrate new processes, and what would a new system do for the ability to grow your business?"

It's that easy. In the example, you don't have to worry about searching for the word "FEEL", simply repeating it back ensures that you are still in the same representational system. People will not notice, and you will build rapport as they interpret you are listening. For longer sentences, simply pick out some key sentences and echo these back and you will achieve the same effect.

Your critical mind may say, "I couldn't possibly do that!" First, try it in a non-business setting and prove to yourself that it works before trying this with customers or clients.

In sales, the more we can shift our thoughts away from internal thoughts and to external awareness, then the greater will be our perceptive skills.

Learning from Watching

I find the easiest way to establish somebody's preferred representational system is to watch rather than listen to them. As visual and kinaesthetic account for the largest proportion of people, so let's concentrate on those. When watching people, we are looking for cluster patterns.

Cluster Patterns

Cluster patterns are patterns of behaviour that can be observed not in isolation but as part of a group of behaviours. Remember, this is not an exact science and what we are looking for are patterns of behaviour that reinforce each other. Some examples of clustering patterns are listed below.

Identifying a Visual

- Speak and talk quickly.
- Move and walk quickly.
- Breathe high in the chest and rapidly.
- Prefer pictures and diagrams rather than written words.
- Looks are important.

- Concerned about the way they look and dress.
- Remember faces easier than names.
- Imaginative.
- Quick decision maker.
- Firm Handshake.

Identifying a Kinaesthetic

- Breathe slower and deeper from the abdomen.
- Move slowly.
- Speak slower.
- Everything is about feel and emotion.
- Often touch when they speak to you.
- Sometimes can stand quite close.
- Like to embrace.
- Longer handshake. Often hold on at the end of a handshake.
- Sometimes have a double handed handshake.
- Softer grip handshake.
- Pause a lot while talking. Speak deliberately.
- Slow decision maker.

How to Communicate With the Different Styles

It's important when communicating with people to realise that it doesn't matter what you think, it's what they think that's important. We must communicate with people in the style that is best for them, not for us. People don't fit neatly into boxes and human communication is complicated. There are going to be people who will display all the traits listed above and there will be others who will have a leaning towards them. The observations are useful indicators and are true enough to be true.

Let's look at two opposing representational systems, visual and kinaesthetic. I fall into the visual category. I like things that look good. I speak, walk, and move quickly and get excited by new ideas, and don't feel too comfortable with physically embracing strangers. Probably the best way to illustrate how to communicate with the different styles would be through a story.

I know someone who is my complete opposite and he would be an extreme kinaesthetic. When we first meet, I prefer a handshake and he prefers an embrace and stands very close. The handshake tends to go on for a bit longer, as does the grip at the end of it. He speaks very slowly and deliberately and takes a long time to get to the point. For a visual like me, I want to press the fast forward button, speed things up and get to the point quickly and in an entertaining way. He would have the opposite point of view and may feel that I was a little cold, impatient, unengaging and not showing enough emotion or feeling.

When a visual is speaking to a kinaesthetic, it is important to slow everything down. This means movement, speech, breathing, and ideas. When describing something, move away from how things look to how they feel. Using phrases as it felt like a good meeting, rather than it looked like a good meeting, will help create a connection.

CHAPTER 4

The Power of Belief

"Whether you think you can or think you can't, you're right."

Henry Ford

In my experience and of observing successful salespeople, many had a strong inner belief. This is a belief that they would achieve their targets and would satisfy the demands that their company had put upon them.

One salesperson that I knew was the top salesperson every year. He didn't have the best area in terms of volumes of business or opportunities and yet always managed to be number one. He was like a magnet attracting business. I remember nearing the end of one sales year and he was still not in the number one position. Then in the last week of December, as if by magic, the number one spot was reclaimed.

It was interesting that the idea of not being number one had not been entertained. His view was that the number one position had not been secured, "yet." This was more than self-belief, it was a knowing!

BELIEF AND PLACEBO

The power of belief has been well documented with research into placebos. The word placebo is of Latin origin and means "I shall please."

Placebos often can masquerade as drugs and look like drugs, but are often no more than sugar pills. Research has been carried out with patients who experienced migraines. Researchers asked all of their subjects to refrain from taking any medication for two hours after the onset of their first migraine. The subjects were then given six envelopes, each containing a pill to be taken during their next six migraine attacks. Two of the envelopes were labelled "Maxalt", a drug used for the treatment of migraines. Two of the envelopes indicated that the pill inside could be either "Maxalt or Placebo." The final two envelopes were labelled "Placebo." Subjects then rated their amount of pain two hours after taking each pill. When subjects took no pills, they reported a fifteen per cent increase in migraine pain after two hours. When they took a pill labelled placebo, they reported a twenty six per cent reduction in pain. When they took a pill labelled as Maxalt, they reported forty per cent reduction in pain.

However, when they took a pill that could have been either a placebo or Maxalt, they also reported a forty per cent decrease in pain. Incredibly, the placebo labelled as Maxalt was equally as effective as the actual Maxalt drug.

A Most Extraordinary Story

One of the most extraordinary stories about the power of belief relates to an article in 1957 in the Journal of Projective Techniques referencing the physician Philip West and his patient, Mr Wright. The story is so extraordinary that had it not been documented in the official Medical Journal, it could have been thought of as pure fantasy.

Mr Wright had an advanced malignancy associated with the lymph nodes known as lymphosarcoma. Mr Wright was under the care of Dr Philip West and was in a terminal state requiring an oxygen mask to assist with his breathing. He had large tumours the size of oranges in his neck, groin, chest, and abdomen. He had between one to two litres (33 to 68 oz.) of milky fluid drawn from his chest every other day.

However, Mr Wright was not without hope. A new drug was being developed called Krebiozen and Philip West's clinic had been chosen by the Medical Association for the evaluation of the treatment. Mr Wright was considered ineligible for the trial because of his short life expectancy of only a few weeks.

When the drug arrived, Wright pleaded with Philip West to be included in the trial. West gave in and agreed to allow Wright to be part of the test. On Friday morning before the treatment, Wright was gasping for air and completely bedridden. The drug was then administered intravenously and Philip West did not see him again until Monday morning.

Upon returning, West was astonished to see Wright up and about and chatting to the nurses without his oxygen mask. Wright's progress had been amazing, and in a matter of days, the tumours had shrunk like snowballs on a hot stove to half of their original size. Observing this, Philip West was eager to check on the other patients who had received the same injection. The other patients showed no change, if anything, they were worse.

The injections continued three times a day and within ten days, Mr Wright was discharged from his deathbed, with practically all signs of the disease having been banished. He was now breathing normally and could fly his plane at 12000 feet (3657 metres) with no discomfort.

After two months, reports started coming out from all the testing clinics that Krebiozen was not effective and that there were no positive results so far. This troubled Wright, and he began to lose faith. After two months of perfect health, he relapsed into his original state.

At this point, Philip West thought there was an opportunity to double-check the drug and took advantage of Wright's optimism to conduct a scientific experiment. West decided to lie to Mr Wright and say that he was not to believe what he was reading in the newspapers and that initial results with the drug had been very promising. He told him that the next day a new version of the drug was arriving, which was a super strength drug.

Philip West waited a few days before administering the drug intravenously in an identical manner. On this occasion, Wright's recovery was even more dramatic. The tumours melted, the chest fluid vanished, and he went back to flying his plane again. However, these injections that Phillip West was administering were not a super strength version of Krebiozen but freshwater!

The final AMA announcement then appeared in the press, stating that Krebiozen was a worthless drug in the treatment of cancer. Within a few days of this report, Mr Wright was re-admitted to the hospital, his faith now gone, and he died in less than two days.

Belief Overriding Genetics

Albert Mason was a young anaesthesiologist who often used hypnotism to treat pain and cure common ailments. This amazing story is documented in the British Medical Journal. The case in 1951 concerns a young boy aged 16 whose skin was covered in black warts except for his chest, neck, and face. The skin was as hard as a fingernail and would crack on the surface and leak blood-stained serum.

In an attempt to help the patient, the boy underwent skin graft surgery. Unfortunately, the two skin grafts were unsuccessful. Mason suggested to one of the surgeons to try hypnosis, as it had been reported as being very successful for curing warts. The surgeon, not amused, said, "Well, why don't you try it!"

Treatment by hypnosis began on 10th of February, 1951. The patient was hypnotised and under hypnosis, a suggestion was made that the left arm would clear. After about five days, the hard layer of skin softened and fell off. Within a few days, the skin became pink and soft. At the end of ten days, the arm was completely clear from shoulder to wrist.

What is remarkable about this story is that the boy didn't have a bad case of warts, but had "congenital ichthyosiform erythroderma" or Brocq's disease, for which there is no cure.

Once Mason discovered that there had been a misdiagnosis and that it was not a case of warts, he was unable to repeat the treatment. His belief had changed.

Surely This Would Never Work

Surgeon J. Bruce Moseley, of the Houston Veterans Affairs Medical Centre, has carried out numerous operations for osteoarthritis of the knee over the years. Osteoarthritis is a loss of essential joint cartilage and can be very painful and debilitating for the person suffering from it. As a remedy, arthroscopic knee surgery is often carried out. Two forms of surgery take place in which,

1. Loose or worn cartilage is cut away.
2. Bad cartilage is flushed out with liquid.

Mosely had organised a study, and his colleagues randomly placed one hundred and eighty osteoarthritis patients into three treatment groups. The first group had surgery in which loose or worn cartilage was cut away. The second group had surgery in which the bad cartilage was flushed out with liquid. The third group had sham surgery. The surgery was carried out as if it was real surgery with an incision made and Mosely even followed a video for authenticity to re-enact the operation to the full.

For two years after the procedures, patients continued to evaluate their knee pain. The results show that at every point in the investigation, all three groups reported an equal degree of reduction in pain and an increase in activity level. Some were so pleased with the sham surgery that they asked for the other knee to be operated on as well. One individual, a Korean War victim, responded so well to the sham surgery that he could play basketball again with his grandchildren after previously requiring a stick to walk.

Overcoming the Poison

The Free Pentecostal Holiness Church is a religious sect located in the mountainous regions of Eastern Kentucky, Tennessee, parts of Indiana and North Carolina. They observe strict practices as part of their everyday life. They attend church frequently and indulge in what some would describe as extreme rituals to display and test their faith.

As part of a test of faith, there have been over two hundred observed instances of successful handlings of poisonous rattlesnakes and copperheads. There were also instances where several different worshippers, during an ecstatic state, handled "fuel oil" torches, acetylene flames, and flaming coal without having either thermal injury to their bodies or clothing.

Two ministers, in a state of exaltation, have been observed to drink toxic doses of strychnine sulphate solution, with no harmful effects.

Your Thoughts Activate Your Genes

Bruce Lipton's pioneering research into the field of epigenetics shows how our thoughts can affect our genes. We are speaking to our genes with every thought that we have. The fast-growing field of epigenetics is showing that who we are is the product of our belief, which changes the way our genes operate.

What does not change is the genes that we were born with, but what does change is the way thoughts affect the hundreds of proteins, enzymes and other chemicals that regulate our cells. Thoughts and beliefs really can affect the outcome.

The Effect of Belief on Others

It is well known that a person's belief in the hypnotist affects the ability to be hypnotised. However, hypnotist and mind control researcher, George Estabrooks, established that the belief of the hypnotist affects the ability to hypnotise the subject.

In medicine, attention is often given to the role that a patient's belief in a particular treatment plays and its efficacy. There is, however, also the question of the Doctor's belief and the effect that it has on the outcome. It has been shown that the Doctor's belief in a particular therapy can, and does affect the outcome for a patient. This has been shown in double blind experiments.

Double-blind studies have been examined by Jerry Solfvin to examine the effect of using vitamin E in the treatment of pain associated with coronary artery disease. One of the doctors in the study enthusiastically believed in the power of vitamin E, while the other three doctors did not. Surprisingly, the results of the double-blind studies matched the doctor's beliefs. The enthusiastic doctor found the effects of Vitamin E to be better than the placebo, while the other two doctors did not.

Solfvin also cites another case. In the 1950s there were conflicting reports about meprobamate, a tranquillizing drug. A double blind study was designed. One of the Doctors administering the drug felt positive and enthusiastic about it and the other was sceptical about whether it would work. Neither the Doctors nor the patients knew whether they were involved with the drug, or the placebo, and did not know that they were part of an experiment. The results for the drug proved more effective for the patients of the enthusiastic doctor, but were no better than the placebo for the sceptical doctor.

In all these stories and studies, something very important has emerged. The power of belief can, in many cases, override reality. The outcome seems to be affected not just by the recipient's belief, but also by the belief of the operator. This is profound and, in a sales context, is worth exploring and thinking long and hard about. Argue for your weakness and it's yours!

THE POWER OF DRIVE AND FOCUS

The Power of Drive

If belief affects the outcome, what are the effects when combined with drive and focus? To illustrate this, let's look at how a sports legend approaches drive and focus.

Scottish rugby legend Chris Paterson is Scotland's record points scorer with 809 points and is the second most capped Scottish player with 109 caps. American football would be a loose equivalent of rugby for those less familiar with the game. As well as being a first class rugby player, Chris is renowned for his kicking accuracy. There is a lot of pressure on the goal kicker, and in many games, the only, or a majority of the points scored are from the boot of the goal kicker. The goal kicker can, therefore, win or lose a game and is under considerable pressure.

Chris started playing rugby at the age of three. Growing up in the town of Gala in the Scottish borders, he was surrounded by rugby and he dreamt of playing for Scotland. Even at this early age, he had already decided that he was going to play international rugby. He realised that to achieve this dream meant a lot of hard work. Wanting to be the best and fittest player in any of the teams that he played for, he trained hard to achieve this.

Chris started goal kicking as a schoolboy. In schoolboy rugby, not much kicking takes place. However, he developed an interest after seeing international rugby on the television. At lunchtime, he would grab some rugby balls, head to the rugby pitch and begin practising kicking the rugby balls at goal.

When kicking for Scotland, Chris worked extensively with kicking coach Mick Byrne, and during this period, Chris' technique changed beyond recognition. The biggest thing Mick Byrne brought was the ability to educate. He explained in great detail what would happen if the left shoulder came out, the left foot was too close, the right leg came up too fast, or the head came up.

Working with Mick, Chris developed and followed the same well rehearsed process every time. The first step was to slow the heart rate down and then run through the preparation step by step.

After a kick has been taken, every kick is evaluated, whether successful or not. If a kick was missed and a second kick was taken from a similar place, the thought of, *"I had better kick this one as I missed the previous one"*, was dismissed as the analysis had taken place and the previous fault identified. Each kick is treated as equally important irrespective of the score in the match. Sometimes a perfectly executed kick can be caught by a gust of wind and will miss. In these circumstances, a kicker can't blame themselves as long as they have gone through their kicking procedure.

The Power of Focus

Many of us, if asked to kick a ball at a target, would simply kick the ball at it. Chris Paterson didn't just look at the goalposts, he picked a small target beyond the goalposts. This could have been the "S" in Scottish Rugby or the "M" on the Murrayfield Stadium sign. This narrowing of focus greatly improved the success rate. The target was then used after the kick in the self-evaluation process to check alignment.

Chris detached from the outcome of each kick, no matter how important and focused on the process. Following the process helped shut out the over eighty thousand people that may be watching live in the stadium. Every kick was treated the same, whether Scotland was thirty five points in the lead or whether it was a kick to win the game. The ball was not struck any harder or any differently.

Many of us, if asked to kick a ball, would have a look at the ball that we were about to kick and then kick it. Chris' attention to the process narrows this down to looking at a small point, which can sometimes be a stitch on the ball.

Such was Chris' dedication that between 11 August 2007 and 7 June 2008, he successfully kicked 36 consecutive goals for Scotland, not missing a single attempt, which was a record at the time. This is a remarkable achievement. What was even more remarkable was that not all the kicks were easy, and this was at a time when Scotland was not a dominant force in world rugby.

Applying to Sales

In sales, we can learn a lot from the discipline that Chris has shown with goal kicking.

1. Follow and trust a process.
2. The importance of focus and having a specific target.
3. Learning to self-evaluate.
4. Ability to engage and learn from others.
5. Accept that some things are outwith of our control.
6. Detaching from the outcome and focusing on the proven process to generate results.

Finally, learning to manage your state if you want to be at your most effective, and we will look at this key ingredient in the next chapter.

Additional Help To Change Your Beliefs

For those looking for some additional help there are specially recorded audio programs including "Supreme Confidence", "Present Like a Pro", and "Charisma on Demand". Simply put on earphones lie back, relax and do nothing.

You do not have to purchase these; they are for those looking for some additional help. Find out more here https://power2mind.com/-nlp-audio

For a 70% discount, use code POWER70.

*Do not use if you suffer from epilepsy or any mental illness.
**No liability is assumed for the use or consequences of any audio program.

CHAPTER 5

Managing Your State

"If you don't control your emotions, they will control you, and that's no good."

Mariano Rivera

One of the real magic ingredients is the ability to control your state. What is meant by state control? This is the ability to control and recall emotions and to use them constructively.

STATE SECRETS

I cannot emphasise enough how important managing your state is. Being able to manage your state is one of the key skills that any communicator or salesperson needs to master.

I am sure that we have all been in a situation when we were about to purchase something and the attitude of the person was less than favourable. This attitude rubs off on us and affects our willingness to buy something. It has been said that enthusiasm is infectious. Let's see if we can draw now on some research to see if there is any evidence for any interconnection between two people.

Getting to the Heart of the Matter

Most of us have been taught that the heart is constantly responding to "orders" sent by the brain as neural signals. However, the heart sends more signals to the brain than the brain sends to the heart. These heart signals have a significant effect on the brain and influence emotional as well as attention, perception, memory and problem solving.

Not only does the heart respond to the brain, but the brain continuously responds to the heart. The heart communicates to the brain in four major ways.
1. Neurologically (through the transmission of nerve impulses).
2. Biochemically (via hormones and neurotransmitters).
3. Biophysically (through pressure waves).
4. Energetically (through electromagnetic field interactions).

All these communication methods affect brain activity. Research from the Heartmath Institute shows that the messages that the heart sends to the brain also can affect performance. The heart is the most powerful source of electromagnetic energy in the human body, producing the largest rhythmic electromagnetic field of any of the body's organs. The heart's electrical field is about sixty times greater in amplitude than the electrical activity generated by the brain. Furthermore, the magnetic field produced by the heart is more than a hundred times greater in strength than the field generated by the brain. This can be detected up to three feet away from the body and has been verified using SQUID-based magnetometers.

Evidence now supports the idea that a subtle yet influential electromagnetic or "energetic" communication system operates just below our conscious level of awareness. The results of these experiments have concluded that the nervous system acts as a type of antenna, which is tuned to and responds to the magnetic fields produced by the hearts of other individuals.

It has been observed that this energetic communication ability can be enhanced, resulting in a much deeper level of nonverbal communication, understanding, and connection between people. This illustrates the importance of state control and its effect on the interaction with others.

The Link between Physiology and Psychology

When people are in an emotionally charged state, their body language reflects this. If someone is angry, for example, they display typical anger body language, such as a narrowing of the lips and furrowing of the brow. The big question is that if your emotions are reflected in your physicality, is this just a one-way process? Would it work the other way around?

Amy Cuddy found that there is a strong link between feelings of power and adopting a power pose. It is not surprising that this takes place because other disciplines, such as yoga, have body positions at their core.

This means that by adopting a different body posture, it is possible to generate a corresponding emotional response. You may have noticed that when somebody is depressed, they tend to look down at the ground and make themselves smaller. Someone who has just had a winning or a victorious moment will often look up, and you may see a clenching or pumping of the fists as they make themselves bigger. This is the body language of victory and success.

If you find yourself feeling depressed, look up with your eyes and notice how it's very difficult to keep that depressed feeling going. Likewise, if you're feeling victorious and you adopt a depressed body language position, it is very difficult to keep that successful feeling going.

Fluidity of State

Being able to move into different states of mind takes a bit of practice. This is something that you can practise away from meetings with customers. It is very useful to shift into different emotional states and in sales, two of the most useful are success and confidence.

People often say that it is not possible to change your state. Yet is that not what actors do when they get into character or when a rock star goes on stage? Imagine winning the lottery. Do you think that your mental state would change?

The easiest way to get into a particular state is to revivify a previous experience as strongly and as realistically as possible. The secret to the success of this is imagination.

It has already been established that the same part of the brain processes something vividly imagined and something real. Let us experiment with this. Pick a time when there are no distractions and immerse yourself as much as you can in the following exercise. You may even want to close your eyes to enhance the experience.

Exercise

I'd like you to think about a lemon and to imagine holding that lemon in your hand. Notice the bright yellow colour and firmness of the lemon as you gently squeeze it, feeling its waxy surface. Bring the lemon slowly up to your nose and breathe in and noticed that faint smell of lemon. Now take the lemon and place it on a cutting board. Reach across, and grab a very sharp knife. Now begin to slowly slice the lemon very gently with the knife and notice how the lemon juice starts to drip gently out from the lemon. You may even hear a sound as the lemon juice escapes. Notice the fresh clean smell of lemon as you breathe in. Keep on cutting so that the lemon becomes in two halves. Now, cut a wedge of lemon. Reach down and grab the wedge of lemon and bring it slowly up to your nose and notice how the smell of lemon gets stronger and stronger the closer it gets to your nose. Continue bringing the lemon up to your nose. Breathe in the fresh, pleasing lemon smell. Now take the lemon and open your mouth and take a big bite.

Many of you will now be salivating. When I have described and used the same story in front of a live audience, many will start to screw their faces up when imagining taking a bite from the imaginary lemon. Of course, there is no lemon, it is purely imaginary. Nonetheless, many of you will have started to salivate, and some of you may even have screwed your face up in anticipation. This shows the power of imagination.

In the previous example, depending on how good your imagination is, will depend on how realistic that experience was for you. The very thought of Indian food has the same effect in terms of salivation with me. Perhaps it does for you too?

Just imagine if you can make yourself salivate and screw your face up at an imaginary lemon. What else are you capable of imagining? Could being successful be one of them?

CONTROLLING THE STATE

Let's take the principles of state control and use them to create the desired state. This takes a bit of practice and the more that you do it, then the easier it becomes. So, let's start.

First, close your eyes and think about a time when you were at your most invincible, your most confident and very best. Make the experience as big as an IMAX screen and remember to experience this as if reliving the experience and seeing it through your own eyes and not sitting in the audience watching. Make the colours bright and bold and turn up the brightness in the image. See what you saw, hear what you heard, feel what you were feeling. Taste what you may have tasted and smell what you may have smelt.

As the images, sounds, smells, feelings, and tastes start to come back, imagine that there is a dial right in front of you labelled experience enhancer. Imagine turning that dial all the way to full. Notice how the feelings intensify and hold the state for about two minutes.

Now open your eyes and think about something fairly ordinary and mundane, like what you had for your dinner last night. Let's repeat the exercise and this time let's really intensify the experience. Repeat the exercise.

Every time we repeat this, which is called fractionation, it deepens the experience. Depending on your level of absorption, will determine how differently you feel when you open your eyes and return to normal. The key to this is to be playful and to resist the temptation to be logical and too literal. The more you practise, the better you will become. Remember to be playful.

Tips for Practicing

There is a tendency, for some, if they are very logical and structured, to force the experience. The key to success is not to try. Just let it happen and be playful. The act of trying often hinders progress. The key to state management is to be immersed in the experience. The brighter and clearer the picture and the more senses that are involved in the experience, then the more vivid the recall of the state becomes. Think playful and just roll with it.

A Fast Method

If you are looking for a simple and fast method, just getting into the habit of developing an intense desire to get to know someone will get you a long way there. When first meeting someone, find out something that you like about them. It may be their clothing, something about them, or something that they have achieved. Focus your attention on the thing that you like, exaggerate the feeling, and keep focusing on it.

Anchors Away

I have had an interest in lifting weights for many years to keep fit and to help keep my strength up. Every year around December and January, in the UK on television, we have the opportunity to see the world's strongest man.

In 2017, Eddie Hall, from the UK, became the world's strongest man for the first time. My youngest son was three at the time and was fascinated with the program and with Eddie Hall. After Eddie had won the competition in 2017, he was booked for a UK tour. As part of the tour, he came to Edinburgh in Scotland where I live. I was lucky enough to have been given tickets as a present for my young son and I to go along. This was a big surprise for my son, as I knew that he would love to meet Eddie.

On arrival, we had our picture taken and our book signed. Bedtime was fast approaching, and it was time for my young son to return home with his mother. I then entered the main hall and joined the other members of the audience and eagerly awaited the arrival of Eddie Hall.

Eddie arrived in the hall shortly after and gave an excellent, informative, and humorous talk about his background, challenges, and achievements. After his talk, there was an opportunity to ask questions. I had been waiting for this opportunity, as I had a specific question in mind to ask him.

In addition to Eddie Hall being crowned the world's strongest man in 2017, he had also achieved the magnificent feat of being the first man to deadlift 500kg or half a ton. For those more familiar with the imperial measurement system, this is 1100 pounds. For anyone who does not frequent the gym, deadlifting 200kg (440 pounds) is very strong. Lifting 500kg (1100 pounds) is just unbelievable! This had previously been thought of as an impossible feat to achieve.

I remember watching this on TV and was amazed to see Eddie achieve the lift. Before the lift, Eddie seemed to be in a strange place mentally. He seemed to be in an unusual state before attempting to and successfully lifting the 500kg. At one point during the lift, it looked like Eddie's eyes were about to pop out and his nose started to bleed. In the end, he collapsed and needed oxygen to aid his recovery. Eddie goes into more details on how this affected him in the days following the lift in his book. I was fascinated by how he had managed to achieve this lift as there were other men, some of whom were bigger than him, that hadn't managed this.

Back at the event, my opportunity to find out more information was coming. I sat there, determined to make sure I asked my question. The previous questions concerned protein shakes, diet and exercise, and now it was my turn. I quickly seized the opportunity and put my hand up. The mic arrived, and the moment had come.

"Eddie, you guys are all big strong guys. How much of what you do is mental and how much of what you do is physical? Eddie's reply was quite surprising. He informed us that, of course, you have to be big and strong, but over 90% of what strongmen do is mental. He then said something quite surprising. He said that he couldn't have achieved the 500kg lift without the aid of a hypnotherapist. The hypnotherapist had told Eddie that he was to pinch the skin on his hand before attempting the lift. Doing this enabled him to get into the state that he needed. It wasn't an angry state, but it was a dark place. This is an example of what we call in NLP (neurolinguistic programming) anchoring.

Anchoring is common in everyday life. When we hear a song, it reminds us of someone; we smell a fragrance and it reminds us of someone. Another example is when we refuse to go back to a restaurant where we experienced a bad meal, even though it was five years ago and the Chef has probably long since gone, together with the offending food.

Mouth Watering

Anchoring first came to prevalence from the work of Ivan Pavlov with his dogs. During the 1890s, Russian physiologist Ivan Pavlov was researching salivation by dogs when being fed. Saliva flow was measured by inserting a small test tube into the cheek of each dog, and saliva was measured when the dogs were fed meat powder.

Pavlov predicted that the dogs would salivate when food was placed in front of them. However, what he observed was that the dogs would begin to salivate whenever they heard the footsteps of anyone who was bringing them the food. This was an important discovery in how we learn.

Pavlovian Conditioning

Pavlov started with the idea that some things are hard-wired into dogs that they do not need to learn. The ability to salivate when they see food being one of them. In behaviourist terms, food is an unconditioned stimulus and salivation is an unconditioned response. This means that it requires no learning. Unconditioned Stimulus (Food) leads to an Unconditioned Response (Salivate).

To explore this further, Pavlov created an experiment. In his experiment, he used metronomes, bells and lights as his neutral stimulus. Pavlov then began the conditioning procedure. He would start the metronome clicking just before he gave food to his dogs. This procedure was repeated until he just started the metronome clicking. As was expected, the sound of the clicking metronome on its own caused an increase in salivation. The association between the metronome and the food had been established and the dog had learnt a new behaviour. This learnt behaviour is a "conditioned response", also known as a "Pavlovian response." For this association to occur and for learning to take place, the two stimuli have to be presented fairly close together in time (such as the metronome and the food). He called this the law of temporal contiguity.

Eddie's Anchor

When Eddie Hall had visited the hypnotherapist, he learnt a conditioned response. The hypnotherapist had helped Eddie to create the state that he wished to have. The desired state was then associated with a pinching of the skin on his hand. This generated the conditioned response or anchor. Just as Pavlov's dogs learnt to associate the sound of a metronome and bell with food, we can learn and bring back our desired state with an anchor. In Eddie's case, this was with a pinch of skin on the hand, but tapping a knuckle works too. It is best to have an anchor that is not too obvious, as we only want to select this when we want to use it.

If this method was effective enough to enable Eddie to lift a previously thought of as an impossible amount of weight, then just think of the power that this could have in your sales and everyday life.

Your Personal Power Anchor

Let's go back to the desired state again. Having practised this a few times, it should get easier now to recall the state. Close your eyes. Think about a time when you were at your most invincible, your most confident, and very best. Make the image as big as an IMAX screen and remember to experience this as if you are reliving the experience and seeing it through your own eyes. Make the colours bold and bright and turn up the brightness in the image. See what you saw, hear what you heard, and feel what you were feeling. Recall any smells or tastes associated with the experience. Imagine seeing a dial that says experience enhancer and turn it all the way up to full. Just as your state starts to peak, either pinch the skin on your hand, or tap one of the knuckles on your hand. Open your eyes and think about what you had for dinner last night. Now repeat the process all over again. Keep doing this exercise a few more times until you have well and truly anchored the state that can be recalled with a pinch of the skin or tap of the knuckle. The degree to which you will achieve success will depend on your ability to fully absorb into the experience. Congratulations, you now have a resource anchor.

REAL OR IMAGINED

Whenever you are learning a new skill, it can take time to master and it is useful to have a fast track method. As already discussed, something vividly imagined and something real are both processed by the same parts of the brain. Could it be possible to imagine a way to succeed? Let's have a look at what the research says.

Imagining Success

Volunteers were asked to play a simple sequence of piano notes each day for five consecutive days, and their brains were scanned each day in the region connected to the finger muscles. Another set of volunteers was asked to imagine playing the notes instead and also having their brains scanned each day. It could be seen that the changes in the brain in those who imagined playing piano notes were the same as those who actually played the piano. This shows that the brain doesn't distinguish real from imaginary!

A study published in the Journal of Neurophysiology found that simply imagining exercise can tone muscle, delay atrophy, and even strengthen the muscles. Researchers at Ohio University conducted an experiment using two groups of "healthy individuals." The researchers wrapped the wrists of one of the groups and set them in casts. They then gave them instructions to sit still for eleven minutes, five days a week, for four weeks, and to perform mental imagery of strong muscle contractions. The other set was not given any instruction.

At the end of the four weeks, the participants who engaged in the "mental exercise" were twice as strong as those who didn't. Those participants had created stronger neuromuscular pathways. Exercising imagery techniques are commonly used by professional athletes to improve performance. However, the university's study is the first to prove that imagery can delay or stop muscle atrophy. The results illustrated that the body and mind are more intertwined than we may have thought.

Basketball Glory

A study conducted by Doctor Biasiotto at the University of Chicago was carried out where he split basketball players into three groups. Each group tested how many free throws they could make. After this, Biasiotto had the first group practice free throws every day for an hour. The second group just visualised themselves making free throws. The third group did nothing. After 30 days, he tested them again and the results are as below:

> The first group improved by 24%
> The second group improved by 23% without touching a basketball.
> The third group did not improve, which was expected.

In a separate study in 1960, Clark, L. V. found that mental practice was nearly as effective as actually practising under the conditions of the experiment.

Steve Nash, the NBA's all-time free throw percentage leader, always takes several imaginary shots before taking the shot. It helps him not only visualise the ball going through the net but also gets his brain and body prepped for the upcoming motor skill. After almost 3400 regular attempts, his 90.4% success rate seems to work.

There seems truth to the statement "You only achieve what you believe."

Why Do We Get Nervous?

One of the most useful states to be able to control is that of being anxious or nervous. Before doing this, let's explore why we get nervous and what happens.

Many processes are carried out beneath our level of awareness automatically by the autonomic nervous system. The autonomic nervous system regulates bodily functions such as heart rate, blood pressure, pupil dilation, body temperature, sweating, and digestion. There are only two processes that can be consciously overridden. One is the blink rate and the other breathing. Within the autonomic nervous system, there are two systems responsible for regulating the organs of the body in response to a stimulus. These are the parasympathetic nervous system and the sympathetic nervous system. The hypothalamus in the brain maintains homeostasis or balance between the two nervous systems.

The parasympathetic nervous system is stimulated when we are at rest, "the rest and digest state." The sympathetic nervous system is stimulated by the fear response at times of stress. The amygdala sends a message to the hypothalamus and, if overstimulated, triggers the fight, flight, or freeze response. This prepares the body for fight or flight by increasing the blood flow to the large muscles and away from the extremities. Breathing becomes shallower, faster, and higher in the chest and the heart rate increases. Non essential systems are shut down and peripheral vision and hearing are reduced and we experience tunnel or foveal vision. The digestive and immune systems also shut down. This results in butterflies in the stomach. Blood drains from the prefrontal cortex, shutting down rational thought. This makes it virtually impossible to learn anything or to focus on small things or engage with other people, as the survival instincts kick in.

Many of us will have had the experience of being under stress and trying to read a page in a book. We can read a passage over and over again and it just won't go in. Think about a heated argument that you had where you didn't say the right things at the time. Then afterwards, as you cool down, thoughts of I wish I had said that occur. Why does this happen? This is because you were not thinking critically.

How to Control the Nerves

We established the link between our state and body and we can do a similar thing with the nervous system. Can we fool the nervous system and flip it to a more relaxed state? Let's look first at breathing.

A Breath of Fresh Air

Recapping what happens when we get nervous or anxious,

1. The breathing rate quickens.
2. Breathing shallows.
3. Breathing occurs higher in the chest.

Something very effective is "box breathing." It comes from the Russian martial art Systema. Breathe in from the abdomen for the count of four. Hold for the count of four. Breathe out for the count of four. Do nothing for the count of four. The easiest way to practise this is to count to four when walking and to use steps to help count.

Seeing Everything

Let's look now at vision. While we don't have conscious control over our pupils, we can change our awareness of what we're looking at. When stressed, vision goes from peripheral to foveal or tunnel vision. When relaxed, we have a much wider peripheral vision. As peripheral vision is associated with a state of relaxation, the nervous system can be tricked back to a more relaxed state by engaging in peripheral vision, or, as Huna practitioners call it, Hakalau. The advantage of this method is that nobody knows that this is taking place, and it is less conspicuous than altering your breathing. Let's try this now.

Pick a point ahead in the distance. Look at that point and then defocus your eyes and start widening your vision. Expand your vision and try to see your ears on either side of your head and to expand your vision. Now try to see behind you. The point that you had been focusing on will start to defocus, but that doesn't matter. What will start to happen is that you will start to relax. It is not advisable to practise this if you're driving a car.

Talking to Yourself

Talking to yourself can be very effective. Scottish Rugby legend Chris Paterson MBE held the record for the highest number of consecutive successful goal kicks (36) in a row at goal without a miss. Chris is well aware of controlling his state. Before any kick, he always allowed his heart rate to slow down. He would talk to himself either under his breath or out loud, reaffirming his beliefs as part of the preparation before taking the kick.

The Alpha Annexe

A method to help you relax is what I call the alpha annexe, and it takes about two minutes. First, find a quiet place. It may even be a cubicle in the bathroom before a meeting. Go in, sit down, close your eyes, and start a progressive relaxation technique. Starting at the head, relax all the muscles in your scalp. Next, relax all the muscles in and around your eyes. Now relax the muscles around your jaw. Move that feeling of relaxation to the muscles around your neck, shoulders, and upper arms. Now relax the muscles around your upper back, chest, lower back, and abdomen. Allow that relaxation to spread to all the muscles around your hips and thighs. Move the relaxation to your lower legs, calves and feet.

When doing this, the brain waves start to change from beta, which is very alert, to alpha, which is a light daydream state. Some people are so used to being in a constant state of stress that they don't know how to relax. Some find it difficult to relax the individual muscles around their body. A method to help with this is to contract and tighten the muscles hard in the area being targeted. Then relax all the muscles. This lets you experience the contrast between tension and relaxation.

CHAPTER 6

Rapport Building

"The single biggest problem in communication is the illusion that it has taken place."

George Bernard Shaw

Rapport is a deep level of communication and understanding between two or more people and is fundamental to any relationship. With rapport, just about anything is possible and without it, very little. Before looking at rapport building, let's examine the science behind rapport, beginning with entrainment.

SWINGING PENDULUMS

In 1666, the Dutch physicist, Christian Huygens, discovered that the pendulum frequencies of two clocks mounted on the same wall or board became synchronised to each other. He surmised that the vibrations of air molecules would transmit small amounts of energy from one pendulum to the other and synchronise them to a common frequency.

However, when the pendulums were set on different surfaces, the effect disappeared. The transmitting medium was the vibrating board or wall. The stronger "oscillator" locks the weaker into its frequency. When both oscillating bodies have equally strong energy, both systems move toward each other. The faster system slows down and the slower system speeds up until they lock into a common movement.

Entrainment

The synchronisation of pendulums can be explained by entrainment. Entrainment is a process through which independent systems interact with each other. When two signals are close to each other in frequency, they fall into a single frequency, just like when the pendulums started to swing in synchronisation.

The phenomenon also extends to the biological world, where examples include those of synchronising fireflies and in humans with the resetting of the body clocks by sunlight (circadian entrainment). The "entraining" signal can be from inside the body or from outside.

Have you ever found yourself walking down the street deep in conversation with someone and then looked down and noticed that your footsteps were totally in sync? This is an example of entrainment. Entrainment is an unconscious process and breathing can become entrained with the beat of the music.

Experiments have shown that when individuals interact socially, for example in conversation, the rhythms of their actions become entrained. It is not merely enough being in the same room, there has to be mutual attention for this to occur. This is implying that there is some sort of connection that connects people and the key ingredient is mutual attention to each other.

BUILDING RAPPORT

When people are in rapport, they often say "we are on the same wavelength." This expression is a good metaphor for considering rapport and there is support for this from the research.

Think about being at the beach or by the sea and consider two waves interacting with each other. If two waves are in sync with each other, then you have constructive interference and the wave becomes larger. In rapport terms, this represents a strengthening of the relationship. If, however, the waves are not in sync, then the peaks and troughs cancel each other out and you have destructive interference. In terms of rapport, this means a destruction of the relationship or no rapport. Using this wave analogy, the closer the two waves are to being in sync then the stronger will be the resultant wave.

What does this mean for rapport? The more you are like somebody then the more rapport you will have with them. A good analogy for this is to think of rapport as a pile of paper on a table, with each component of rapport represented by a single sheet of paper. A single sheet of paper on its own is very flimsy and is not solid. You could blow on the piece of paper and it would move. Imagine meeting somebody for the first time and you find out that they are from the same town as you. This would represent a single layer of rapport or sheet of paper in our analogy. You then find out that you went to the same school. This represents another layer or sheet of paper in our analogy. You find out that you have similar hobbies and political leanings.

These additional things in common represent additional layers of rapport, just like adding more sheets of paper to the pile. The more sheets you add to the pile, the stronger it becomes. This is the same with rapport and I call this layering. Just as the pile gets stronger, then so does the level of rapport.

I like to consider four types of rapport.

1. Content Rapport.
2. Non Content Rapport or Physical Rapport.
3. Secret Rapport.
4. Timing Rapport.

Content Rapport

Content rapport includes things that we have in common. This includes interests, background, home town, life experiences, etc. Here we are looking to become as alike as the other person we are talking to as we possibly can. In discussions, we are looking for areas of commonality and not areas of difference. Look for areas of similarity such as music tastes, hobbies, and places of origin, films, sport, and food. A useful tip is that if you discover and share an unusual interest, then this builds massive rapport. For example, if you collect beer cans, or collect corks and someone has the same interest as you, this will build massive rapport.

Always avoid areas of contention. For example, if you discover the person has a political persuasion that is not in line with yours, avoid that subject and change it. Focus on what you have in common, look for more, and avoid what you don't have in common. We must use correct questioning techniques to elicit this information. These are expanded upon in the section on questioning.

Physical Rapport

With physical rapport, we are looking to be as similar to other people as we can in the way that they move, speak, and look. There are a lot of factors at play when trying to build physical rapport, and what we need is a method that makes things easier.

There are two methods, one is an unconscious and the other is a conscious approach. The more physically we can be like someone, then the more rapport we will have with them.

Mirroring and Matching

There are many ways that we can mirror and match. We can match body language, voice (tone, pace, volume, and choice of words) together with breathing and blinking. In this section, we are going to be focusing on physical and vocal mirroring.

Physical Mirroring

One of the fastest ways to build rapport with somebody is to adopt a similar body language. People that are in rapport have similar body language to each other. We can witness this in social situations and by observing people in restaurants, bars, and cafes. It's like a dance and is done at an unconscious level.

Once aware of this, you will start to notice how people lean towards each other, adopt similar body positions, and then mirror each other. When people first discover and become aware of mirroring, it is often a major revelation.

There are three methods for doing this.

1. Mirroring.
2. Matching.
3. Cross matching.

Mirroring

Mirroring is copying somebody's body language just as if looking at ourselves in a mirror. If somebody raises their right hand, then to mirror them, we would raise our left hand. Mirroring is very common in both social and business situations when rapport is present.

Matching

Matching is a form of mirroring done as if standing behind someone rather than facing them. When matching someone, if their right hand is raised, then our right hand would also be raised. I prefer using mirroring as this occurs naturally and unconsciously, but matching works too.

Cross Matching

With cross matching, the body language is matched not directly but covertly. An example would be if the other person is moving their foot up and down, we would raise our finger up and down at the same tempo.

A Word of Caution

When people first discover and become aware of mirroring and matching, they fall into two groups. The first group thinks I couldn't possibly use mirroring or matching because people are going to spot me. They feel uncomfortable and self aware and are reluctant to do it. The second group embraces mirroring and matching quite literally. They think that they have discovered a panacea and decide to go all out and copy somebody's every move, and consequently come across as false.

Let's address these points. We already mirror other people. It is a natural process, but we are often not aware of it. For much of the time, this is outwith conscious awareness. The best way to start mirroring somebody is to have a genuine desire to get to know them. As you develop rapport, automatic mirroring will take place. However, to help get the process started, the best way to practise is in a social situation to satisfy your critical mind that it works. Then, when feeling comfortable with this, it can be incorporated into the business environment.

When I first discovered the idea of mirroring, I was sceptical and wondered if it would work. I was once in a bar with a client and noticed that we were both leaning against the bar. We were facing each other with our bodies slightly angled towards the bar. I spotted that we were both mirroring each other and decided to test mirroring and increased the angle of my body to the bar. To my surprise, the person that I was speaking to, not long afterwards, copied me. Wanting to test this further, I then increased the angle even further, and again, this was copied by the other person. I was stunned by this. It had worked just exactly as I had been told it would.

Using Mirroring

When going into a meeting with a client or a customer, one of the quickest and best ways to build rapport quickly is to mirror the body position of the customer. Even walking at the same pace with steps synchronised develops rapport.

Start by copying the way somebody is sitting or is standing. The idea is to subtly copy their body language. If someone suddenly starts scratching their head, the idea is not to start immediately scratching your head. If you are speaking to somebody and they change their body position by leaning back, a good rule is to wait six seconds before you then change your body position to mirror or match theirs. This will be subtle enough without appearing clunky.

As you get better at this, you will find that you do this easily. This will begin to flow much more naturally and will then become an unconscious response. We will be exploring nonverbal clues more in Chapter 15.

Vocal Mirroring

As well as physically mirroring people, it is also possible to auditorially mirror them. When people speak, many have their favourite words. These are words that they will use that are almost like a catchphrase. If you pick up on these and reflect these back to them, this builds rapport. We have already covered the "echo technique" in Chapter 3, and this is an excellent method for vocal mirroring. Aside from mirroring the actual words, it is possible to mirror the way that people speak. Have you ever changed your accent slightly or the way that you speak when in the company of others? If so, this is a form of mirroring. When people speak, there is the volume, pace, tone, timbre, expression, and emotion that is conveyed in their voice. Volume, pace and emotional expression are important to pay attention to and reflect back to them.

Secret Rapport

A very powerful way to build rapport and trust with somebody is to share a secret. I'm not advocating that you share company secrets, but there may be a piece of information that you could share. Sharing a secret will often cause people to lean forward as their curiosity is aroused.

Reputational risk is important and telling mistruths or making things up will do your relationship and reputation no good. If there is information that you can share with the customer, which is not detrimental to your company, sharing this will build rapport and trust. It is always worth checking with your company that your company would not object to. On a personal level, sharing a personal secret is very powerful in gaining trust and making friends with people.

Timing Rapport

The best way to illustrate timing rapport is by using an example. Have you ever had a situation where you've met somebody, got on very well and said we must meet up for a coffee or a drink sometime? The other person agrees and is keen to do so. Time then moves on and the memory of that person fades and it starts to feel a little uncomfortable to get in touch. The longer we leave it, the worse it becomes. The same thing works with dating. The next meeting must take place, fairly shortly afterwards, to continue developing the relationship.

I liken this to seeds in a garden. If you plant seeds, some of them may grow. However it is more than likely that you will have to look after the seeds to make sure that they are not harmed by frost or eaten by the birds. We also have to make sure that the seeds receive the correct amount of water and that the correct temperature is maintained. There is quite a lot of work involved in the early stages to make sure that they survive. Then, as the seed develops into a plant, it's just the case of a bit of pruning now and again. Think about somebody you've known for many years. You don't have to see them all the time for the relationship to continue. That's because you have established deep roots with them in the first place. Another thing to be aware of is that people formulate their relationships based on common interests. As soon as those interests start to differ or drift apart, the relationship can break down. You may have heard the phrase "growing apart."

The Big Secret

The most effective method in building rapport and the most natural is to develop a deep, strong desire to get to know and build rapport with another. This relies on getting into the correct state and allowing the unconscious mind to do its magic.

When using this method, it's not enough to be friendly and hope that rapport occurs. There must be a strong desire to get to know the person. This begins by changing your state. When doing this, then all the signals of wanting to develop rapport will be shown. You will appear congruent, and this is all done at an unconscious level. If the intentions and the thoughts are right, then the words and all aspects of your voice, and your body language will reflect this.

This is my favoured method and in my opinion, the most powerful. It is also important to be familiar with conscious rapport to spot when it is present and when it has broken down.

CHAPTER 7

Getting People To Like You

"A great man shows his greatness by the way he treats little men."

Thomas Carlyle

Getting people to like you is another part of stacking. Many people decide whether or not they like us within the first few seconds. Research has been carried out with people conducting job interviews. They were instructed within the first minute to write down what they thought of the candidate for the job. They then interviewed the candidate for half an hour and were instructed to write their thoughts down again. What they found was that they hadn't changed their mind.

Being liked is not essential when selling a product or service, but it is a lot more pleasant if you like the individual. If the product or service is a market leader, unique and you want it, then the salesperson is less important. However, most companies are not in this situation and therefore stacking becomes important. Likeability becomes more important for an ongoing relationship with a customer or client. After all, who wants to spend time with people that they don't like? Let's now explore the principles that work best to achieve this.

Pleased to See You

Much of what we do in life is down to modelling, that is, finding what is working for someone else and doing the same. I first unintentionally came across modelling when at school. I remember there was one person who was very popular and had a lot of friends. This individual was always at the centre of everything. Even at a young age, I began wondering how did he have so many friends and was so influential. Then it dawned on me. Whenever he met other people, he always seemed pleased to see them. It didn't matter who it was; they were all greeted in the same way. This is a good habit to adopt.

Think about how excited a young child is or how your pet dog reacts upon seeing you. How good is it when someone is genuinely pleased to see you and compare this to when someone looks like they couldn't care less whether or not you are there?

The Power of the Smile

Psychologist Paul Ekman, in the 1980s, noticed that when studying faces that signalled sadness and distress, he felt terrible afterwards. Ekman and his colleagues monitored the way that their bodies changed and found markers that showed that the sad expressions changed their autonomic nervous system as if they were actually sad themselves.

Smiling Can Lift Your Mood

When smiling or when we see another person smile, we feel happier. Just the simple act of smiling triggers a rush of positive neurological activity, which lowers stress and uplifts moods. Dopamine increases our feelings of happiness and the release of serotonin reduces stress. Having low levels of serotonin are associated with depression and aggression.

On a surface level, we're more prone to reciprocate what we see around ourselves and mirror that internally. Neuroscientist Marco Iacoboni explains that when we see people smiling, our mirror neurons fire up too. This initiates a cascade of neural activity that evokes the feeling we typically associate with a smile. We don't need to infer what someone is feeling; we experience it, just in a milder form.

Genuine Smile

Researchers have discovered that humans have a fake and real smile. A real smile appears primarily because of the action of two muscles: the *zygomaticus major,* which stretches from the corner of the mouth to the cheekbone, and the *orbicularis oculi,* which surrounds the eye. When these two muscles work together, the corners of the mouth are drawn up and a crinkling around the outer edges of the eyes occurs, causing crow's feet. It is important to avoid a false business smile and to make sure that your smile is genuine, and practice if necessary.

Giving Sincere Compliments

Everybody likes to be praised. Think about the look on a young child's face when you praise them. Compare this to the reaction when someone gives negative criticism. Very few people bother to give praise in everyday life and when it does happen, it often takes people by surprise. There is a difference between genuine praise and flattery.

Genuine praise is a recognition of appearance, something achieved, or something about someone. If it is something that someone would like to have acknowledged, then it becomes even more powerful. Everybody has something about them that can be genuinely praised. Compliments can include the choice of clothing, a liking of something that they own or have done, the way a speech was delivered, or perhaps how a meeting was handled.

It is important when giving compliments to be congruent and appear as if you believe it. When people first start giving compliments, they are often surprised by the reaction of the recipient. In many cases, they light up like a Christmas tree. Just observe someone's body language after giving a compliment and notice how their whole demeanour changes.

Don't Criticise

Just as everybody likes to be complimented, nobody likes to be criticised. While criticism can be both positive and negative, criticism has a negative connotation. When being negatively criticised, the natural tendency is to defend our position. People always resist challenges to what they believe to be true and what they think about themselves. Reality is not uniform and is particular to each person, and therefore we are all correct in our mind. Understanding this makes us realise that there is little point in engaging in an argument, as people resist what they are told and accept what they conclude. Arguing with somebody, with strong convictions, is akin to telling somebody that the door is blue when they perceive the door to be green. Vision serves as a good example to show the interpretation of reality because people do perceive colours differently. Some men are colour blind and a small proportion of women are tetrachromats, and can see different colours!

Sometimes genuine feedback will be requested. I have worked in large companies where it was highlighted that the organisation is not a meritocracy and there is not a monopoly on ideas. They stated that genuine criticism and feedback, together with a wide variety of views, are encouraged. This often means, "I want you to give genuine feedback and criticism as long as this is identical to my thinking!" People who are aware of the effect of criticism will always tread carefully here.

A very useful technique is the "criticism sandwich." This involves first highlighting something that the person did very well or achieved. This is usually something that the person would probably know that they did well. In the second part, we move on to the criticism or areas for improvement. In this section, substitute the word "and" for the word "but." "But" acts as a stop word and discounts everything before it. The word "and" links two concepts and allows them to flow. Notice the difference in the sentences below:

> "The concert was good but it was loud."
> "The concert was good and it was loud."

The best thing to do is to avoid criticism wherever possible and to focus instead on the positive aspects of what the person did well.

Don't Complain

One of the golden rules is, "don't complain." People just aren't interested. We have all come across people who, when asked how they are, start listing a series of problems and this can feel like our energy is being sapped. The social norm when meeting somebody is to ask, *"How are you?"* The reply is usually an unconscious response. *"Fine, thanks."* We don't expect people to start listing all their problems one by one. Many people have problems and if somebody lists one particular issue, that's fine, as long as it is brief, but no one wants to hear a list. When somebody asks how you are, it's better to focus on positive aspects and to make it brief. This is particularly important in sales. I once heard a salesperson listing all the problems that they had with a customer. Many of those were related to the company that they were supposed to be representing! Remember that people create their reality based on an impression, and adopting this approach is going to do little to enhance success.

Be Careful When Being Positive

Back in the 1990s, personal development was becoming very popular. A particular theme at that time was the power of positive thinking. I remember being at a sales meeting where this was being discussed and someone said: "That will never work!" I still find that amusing to this day.

Being positive is important, but not overly positive. Overly positive people can come across as annoying. The reason is that others rarely like to hear from someone where everything is perfect in their life because it reflects on the aspects of their own life that are not.

Be aware of cultural differences. Some cultures appreciate a more upbeat approach, while others prefer discretion. I remember one very successful salesperson saying, "magnificent", to everyone anytime that he was asked how he was. This lacked authenticity.

Measured Positivity

It is important to be positive, and it should be measured. A tip that you can use is what I call "measured positivity." If someone asks you how you are, admit to some minor problem or issue before being positive.

> "How are you doing?"

> "Great thanks, the new product launch was slow to begin with and I was under pressure, but now that the customers have seen the benefits of the new IT system, the orders are just flooding in."

This keeps things realistic and more conversational. Do not say that nobody is buying your product, ever!

A good habit to get into immediately is to stop complaining across all parts of your life. An expression that is worth adopting is "don't complain, don't explain."

Make the Other Person Feel Important

Everybody likes to feel important and valued. It doesn't matter what job you are doing; everybody likes to be recognised. People just can't help but warm to people that make them feel important. Referring to what a person does and acknowledging how significant their role is conveys importance to somebody. An individual may say that their role is not very important and all that they do is make sure that the orders go out on time. Reframing this changes the meaning. Simply commenting that their role sounds like an important role because if the orders were late, this would have a detrimental effect on business profitability reframes the role. Develop the habit of making people feel important and you will have a dramatic effect on how they regard you.

How to Win an Argument

The best way to win an argument is to avoid one. In the section on how the brain creates reality, it was explained that each person has their own map of the world and, with it, their own version of reality. Once realised, it is easy to see that there is little point in arguing with somebody to persuade them that your map is better than theirs.

People will resist what they are told and will accept what they conclude. When I see politicians arguing, I just laugh because they are both correct based on their map of reality.

Develop and Show a Real Interest in Other people

Most people's favourite topic of conversation is themselves and many don't listen to what others are saying because they are too busy thinking about what to say next. Simply showing an interest and asking someone about themselves can have a profound effect. The more that you can get people talking about themselves, then the more they are going to like you. This doesn't mean interrogating somebody, but developing a genuine interest to find out more about them. The proper use of questions is covered later in this book. An excellent summary is, if you want to be thought of as interesting, then be interested.

The Magic Word

There is a magic word, a word that is so powerful that it makes people respond. It's a word that when people hear it, makes every one of us feel good. What is this magic word? It's our name. The very mention of our name across a crowded room will instantly cause us to turn round. When our name is used in a conversation, it makes us feel good. Think about all the monuments, buildings, and companies that are named after people. A coincidence perhaps, I think not.

There is an even greater power than hearing your name, and that is if someone remembers your name and uses it. How many times are we introduced to somebody, then immediately, we forget their name? People who can remember other people's names are often perceived as charismatic and very likeable. What is needed is a method to assist with this. There are several memory methods, but they can be quite complicated and can take quite a bit of practice.

A story that I still find amusing is when someone I know with a terrible memory, or rather poor recall, decided to do something about it. He bought a book and excitedly called me, explaining that he had bought this fantastic new book on improving your memory. He was raving about it. I was curious to learn more and asked as to who had written it, and he replied:

"Eh, I can't remember!"

Some memory methods can be quite complicated and require practice. A simple method can make things easier. We learn through repetition and can draw on this to help remember names. When somebody first says their name, immediately repeat it with your internal voice. Then repeat their name back to them out loud with an inflection at the end of the sentence, as if asking a question. Finish off by saying "It's nice to meet you" and then repeat their name.

Let's look at an example of this. Suppose that I meet somebody and his name is Mike. We normally reach out our hand, introduce ourselves and say our name. Here, I would say

"Derek, pleased to meet you."

They would then say their name, for example,

"Mike."

As soon as they say their name is Mike, I repeat,

"Mike", inside my head.

I then verbally repeat their name back to them with an inflection, as if asking them a question, and say,

"Mike?"

They would say *"Yes."*

I would then say, *"Pleased to meet you Mike."*

This allows us time to have heard and repeated their name four times.

The final layer to add to help us remember is to notice if their name reminds us of anything or anyone. In this case, we could imagine a large microphone coming out of Mike's head and create a crazy illogical image to remember this by. If nothing comes to mind, don't worry, this is just an additional step.

Don't Overuse the Name

A word of caution when using somebody's name. Overuse of a name can have a negative effect. If overused, it starts to become more of an annoyance than a relationship builder. This is often associated with the stereotypical high pressure salesperson who realises the importance of somebody's name and yet fails to understand the subtlety of use.

There is not an exact formula as to how many times a person's name should be used in a conversation. It should be interspersed naturally. Let's give an example of overusing somebody's name.

> *"It's great, David, that you have an interest in antiques. Many of our clients have developed a keen interest in the antiques market, David. There are several areas that we could look at, David. Which areas are most appealing to you?"*

This would come across as using somebody's name a bit too frequently. Practice using somebody's name in conversations to build rapport and intersperse naturally.

Avoid Being a Hijacker

A way to destroy rapport and avoid being liked is to become a conversation hijacker. These are people who join other people's conversations uninvited and then promptly start to take over the conversation. This can take place both in a social setting and in a work environment. This often takes the form of *"Yes and I..."* and they start to talk about themselves.

Avoid the tendency to hijack other people's conversations unless invited to join in. A sharpening of awareness will soon let you know if it was welcome.

Dealing with People That You Don't Like

There are always going to be people in life that we are less keen on or get on less well with. These may be people whose values or beliefs oppose ours, or where there is little commonality. We have to be careful because nonverbal signals are displayed and picked up unconsciously.

A method that I have found useful is instead of focusing on differences, focus on what you like about them. If it is difficult to find something positive in their values, examine their personality, something that they are wearing, something achieved, or how well they run their business. This forms part of reframing and while the person is still the same, they are looked at in a new way.

CHAPTER 8

Different Personalities

"Personality is like a charioteer with two headstrong horses, each wanting to go in different directions."

Martin Luther King, Jr.

Personality types have been around a long time. Hippocrates called these the four temperaments and established the four archetypes of people's personalities.

This has evolved and more recently Myers-Briggs, as an adaptation of the theory of psychological types produced by Carl Gustav Jung, has produced 16 personality types. This relies on filling in a questionnaire to identify the different types. While this information is useful, it is just not practical to give a questionnaire to a client or customer and then ask them to fill it in. A method is needed where we can use our observational and awareness skills instead.

IDENTIFYING A PERSONALITY

My favoured method is the Merrill-Wilson model. It is simple to understand and fast to identify. The four personality types are Driver, Expressive, Amiable, and Analytical.

There are two main variables to identify a personality type. Are they better with facts & data or relationships? Are they introverted (low assertion) or extroverted (high assertion)? From this, we get four main types.

Dominant
Fact Based, Extrovert, High Emotional Control.
Analytical
Fact Based, Introvert, High Emotional Control.
Amiable
Relationship Based, Introvert, Low Emotional Control.
Expressive
Relationship Based, Extrovert, Low Emotional Control.

People will move between these boxes in different situations and can be any of the four, but will tend to feel more comfortable in one. The archetype that people fall into is easy to recognise once it is known what to look for.

The Clues

The first step is to identify whether somebody is an introvert or extrovert. Having done that, then pay attention to the warmth of the greeting that you get and this will give you an indication of whether emotional thinking will influence decisions or not.

Dominant - Aim to be in control

Dominant people exhibit control and power. They will often have their calls screened and often don't greet people personally. They tend to be more formal in business and are often dressed more formally. Personal details are often guarded. They often display a firm handshake, direct eye contact and controlled body language with little blinking of the eyes. The body language reflects control and dominance and they don't move much, and when they do, it is with purpose. Hands are often placed on the hips to make themselves bigger with body positions that include standing upright to appear taller with their head back. There is little small talk and they like to get to the point and don't suffer fools gladly. They are tidy, organised and think before speaking, while not being afraid to challenge or to be blunt. A dominant can come across as quite cold, confrontational and argumentative. They like participatory sports rather than spectator sports, and rules are made for others to follow. Being in charge is a must, and they often display a large ego. They can come across as lacking empathy, driven, and competitive. Dominants have a low attention span and are annoyed by slow decision-makers. Efficiency is important and they hate wasting time. Decisions are based on facts and not emotion.

Expressive - Aim to be noticed

An expressive often greets personally with a warm greeting and likes to show people around the business, and will make introductions to colleagues. They display an enthusiastic handshake and are less formal; they are friendly and warm but are not afraid to say no. They often dress extravagantly and love excitement and socialising. They display high energy levels and have frequent direct eye contact, which is less of a stare. They love stories and sharing them. Expressives are talkative, fun, and will usually share everything that is going on in their life, happily discussing their holiday and interests. The subject of conversation often changes quickly, as they jump between topics of conversation. Their voice is expressive and they speak quickly with a high eye blink rate. An expressive's body language incorporates a lot of movement including hand gesturing. They are not well organised and are not very good at follow up. Poor time discipline and an untidy desk are trademarks. They love spectator sports and often have pictures of the family on the wall. Rules are for interpretation. They have a low attention span and are annoyed by excessive detail and slow decision-makers. Decisions are based on emotion.

Amiable - Aim to blend in

Amiables are introverts. They aim to please and dislike confrontation and will often see both sides of the argument. They will greet you personally, are often softly spoken with a warm voice. They are agreeable and reliable and display a soft handshake. They are trusting and want everyone to get along. Their body language reflects being introverted, and they tend to make themselves smaller by keeping their arms and legs under control and close to the body. Amiables hate confrontation and they want people to get along. They like routine and often live in the same area without moving. It's all about relationships, but it takes them a while to get to know and trust people. They build up relationships with the environment as well as people. Buying cars and the pressure associated with it is their worst nightmare. There are few in management positions. They are generally happy but have a tough time refusing people. Amiables make good friends and are good listeners with long attention spans. Rules are to be followed but with consideration for people. They often take on too much work, as they can't say no. They are slow decision makers and are suspicious of fast decision makers, and can come across as indecisive.

Analytical - Aim to work things out

Analyticals love data, details and spreadsheets. They often walk with their head leaning forwards. They are curious and are fascinated by analysis. They will often greet with a soft handshake and without much eye contact. Their voice can often lack expression and can sound quite mechanical and cold. They love detail and can never get enough information. They will know the names of streets, road and flight numbers together with bizarre numerical and historical facts. They can appear cold. They are very precise and will quote exact numbers. Typically, they work in an analytical profession, such as an analyst, accountant, or engineer. Structure is important and they hate chaos. Analytics believe that situations can be managed just with information. They are disciplined with time and figures. They love processes, structure, and procedure. They enjoy a well-structured project. Often, they have low awareness skills and like intellectual hobbies, where detail is important including computers and computer related information. Rules are to be followed to the letter. They have a long attention span

Different Personalities

and are suspicious of fast decision makers. Decisions are made using data.

Type	Strengths	Weaknesses
Dominant	Determined Decisive Independent	Lack of Empathy Impatient Domineering
Expressive	Communication Enthusiastic Creative	Disorganised Talkative Unfinished work
Amiable	Diplomatic Supportive Loyal	Not assertive Reactive Change resistant
Analytical	Thorough Disciplined Structured	Rigid Unemotional Perfectionist

Table 1

Changing Styles

Remember to adapt your presenting styles to fit in with the different personality types. If you are an expressive interacting with an analytical, reduce the enthusiasm and slow your speech down. Remember to include lots of detail. Expect a slow decision and a request for more information.

If you are an amiable presenting to a dominant, avoid too much small talk, get to the big idea quickly and be decisive in your recommendation. Demonstrate what is in it for them, in a logical manner and avoid too much detail.

If you are an analytical presenting to a dominant, remember to get to the point and talk about the big idea generally. Avoid explaining the data in detail but summarise the conclusion of the data and what it means. Expect a quick decision.

If you are a dominant communicating with an expressive, remember to get involved in small talk and show an interest in them. Use exciting stories to illustrate the point, expect to have to listen a lot and bring the conversation back to the topic. Add enthusism to your presentation, speak quicker, relax and let go.

These are generalisations and people will display some, but not all, of the character traits. People will also identify with different styles at different times. However, they will have a box that they identify most with.

PART TWO

Successful Sales Methods

CHAPTER 9

The Truth About Sales

"Our greatest weakness lies in giving up. The most certain way to succeed is always to try just one more time."

Thomas Edison

When thinking of sales, it can very often have negative connotations. Images of pushy people, more interested in selling a product or service that is in their interest rather than satisfying our needs, often come to mind. Yet some salespeople can guide us effortlessly towards the products and services in a nonthreatening and non-pushy way. When this occurs, it makes the process easier, simpler, and more comfortable.

ADVANCED COMMUNICATORS

Sales is no more than an advanced form of communication. The sharper the awareness and communication skills are, then the better someone will be at communicating and persuading people.

Inside the Mind of Sales

Some people look down their noses at salespeople, but everybody is in sales. If in a restaurant and the waiter is asked what dish he recommends and he then steers us towards a particular dish, is this not just sales? If we want to get our children to go to bed on time, the idea has to be sold. If we want to persuade our partner to go on holiday to a particular destination, we must sell the idea to them.

My view of sales is that if a product or service is recommended, then it should be in the interest and for the benefit of the other person. If trying to persuade your partner to go on a rock climbing holiday and they hate rock climbing, would this be fair?

Then there is the question of is it ethical to sell something that you know is not the best in the market? It is an interesting question. Rarely is there one product that is so much better than another and at the same price. If in a clothes shop and you spot a jacket that you like, you wouldn't expect to be informed that there is a jacket next door that is cheaper and of better quality. A salesperson's job is to recommend from the range of offerings to fit in with a customer's needs. Has the person been better off for deciding to use your product or service? If so, then the need has been satisfied. You are not offering a price comparison service.

Suppose that you are selling life insurance and you know that there is life insurance cheaper elsewhere. Is the person going to complain if they could have bought it cheaper when a payout occurs? You have helped them and by being there to help them in the future, what price can be put on this?

DIFFERENT TYPES OF SALES

There are many types of sales situations. Let's look at some of the different types.

B2C

B2C means business to consumer. In this type of situation, the decision maker is being spoken to directly, and it is unlikely that there is a decision making committee. The decision making process is often quicker and the relationship less formal.

B2B

B2B means business to business. There are many types of business to business scenarios. When dealing with smaller businesses, the decision making process can often appear less structured but can be quicker. When dealing with bigger businesses, things progress but very slowly. However, it is rewarding when gaining the order.

The biggest challenge in business to business sales is to make sure to speak to the correct person. This would be the person who is in a position to ultimately decide. Understanding the process for decision making and who is involved is crucial.

Can You See It Feel it or Touch It?

As well as the different sales relationships, there are also different offerings. There are products that we can experience through our five senses, which are tangible offerings. These will include stationery, wine, perfume, flowers, clothing, property or real estate, cars, boats and many more. These can be experienced through the primary senses. This means that the customer can actually see what they will be purchasing and it allows them to experience it before purchase.

Intangible products or services cannot be experienced at the point of sale. This includes a promise to do or offer something in the future. There is no immediate external experience of the product or service and the benefits have to be imagined. This would include investment, insurance, training programmes, advertising, and holidays or vacations. This means that when selling intangibles, the customer or client must be encouraged to internalise the experience and vividly imagine the benefits.

Me Too Sales

With this type of sale, the aim is to substitute what the customer is currently using with our offering. We are trying to persuade the customer or client that what we have is different, or better than what they are currently using. This can have a shorter lead in time as they are already using the product or service and have already identified the need.

The challenge when presenting this solution is that the customer may have loyalty to a particular brand, person, or business and introducing a new product or service can be met with resistance.

Behavioural Change

This type of sale involves asking the customer to do something new or to buy something new. If it is new, they will want to know who else is buying it. This type of sale has a longer lead in time as people are creatures of habit and prefer to buy products or services that have been endorsed by other people.

The advantage is that the competition tends to be less and there is no legacy, personal, business, or brand loyalty issues to deal with.

One Off

This is where there is an opportunity to sell only one product with little opportunity for a repeat sale in the short term. This type of sale would include double glazing, property, or real estate.

Repeat

This involves repeat sales or account management. This type of sale involves an additional skill set. Besides obtaining the customer or client, there is a requirement to service and look after them in the future. This role can often be an account management role. The more contact points that you have with a customer and client then the more opportunities there are to build rapport. This is important for this type of relationship.

RADIO STATIONS AND TRUTHS

Which Radio Station Are You Tuned To?

Everybody is tuned to radio station WIIFM. In other words, "What's in it for me?" If the solution doesn't have an immediate benefit for the person you're speaking to, it's unlikely to have any resonance.

Four Hard Truths

The four truths are:

1. The customer is not interested in you or your product, but what you or it can do for them.
2. People buy with emotion and justify with logic.
3. People buy what they want rather than what they need.
4. People respond better to having a pain removed, or a problem solved than getting better at something.

Even the most altruistic people always look at themselves in a group photograph, before looking at others. Rapport can be built with people if you have a genuine desire to get to know them, however, if you don't have a solution to their pain point or have something that can help them achieve something, then whatever you are presenting will not have the desired effect. If we are suffering from back pain, what we seek is relief from the pain. The product is not important. We want to know what the product can do to relieve the pain.

We all like to think that we are logical. However, many of the decisions are made at the emotional level and justified by logic. For example, that two-door convertible red sports car is practical for going to the shops and running the kids around in, isn't it? What about those red-soled high heel shoes? They are practical for walking around in, aren't they? Why then do people make such purchases? The answer is simple. They make us feel better, more successful, and ultimately more attractive.

Wants and Needs

We focus more on the things that we want, rather than the things that we need. This is because we derive more pleasure from something wanted than needed. Imagine having the choice between a dream holiday or a vacation and replacing the worn out sofa. The chances are that the holiday would win unless your sofa was in such a poor condition as to be unusable.

We respond more to having a problem solved than we do by becoming better at something unless that involves attracting people. You will have more success in helping someone overcome a fear of public speaking than you will from trying to make them a better public speaker.

Swinging the Pendulum

Just as the glass can be half full or half empty, we live in a world of opposites, and the only reason that something exists and is perceived is because of its diametric opposite. Light would not exist if there was no darkness. Therefore, the glass can be described as being half empty, or half full and both would be correct.

People can look for reasons to use a product or service or for reasons not to. Using a pendulum as an analogy, in sales, all we're trying to do is to swing the pendulum from the customer looking for reasons not to use us, our product or service, towards using us, our product or service.

Reasons to Use   Reasons Not to Use

Fig.4

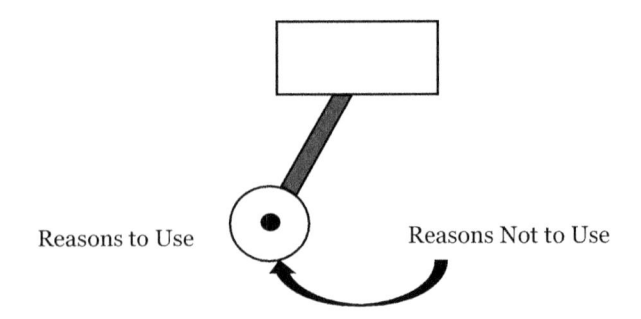

Establishing the Need

One of the most important principles to learn is that people will resist what you tell them and accept what they conclude. If I were to push or pull you, there would be a natural physical resistance to this.

There is also the same principle at work when verbally telling or forcing someone. It's what I call the "F You" principle. Even though you know that the person is correct, there is a part of you going "F you!" Somebody may be forced into a decision by applying pressure, however, buyer's remorse often sets in and the person then experiences resentment. This does little to create any long lasting relationship with a client or customer and certainly does little to build any rapport.

The best type of approach is a consultative approach, where the person is ultimately asking you what they should do. They should not feel that they are being forced down a particular route or path that is in the salesperson's self interest and against theirs.

NUMBERS AND RATIOS

The Numbers Don't Lie

Good salespeople keep a track of their numbers. These include how many sales calls to appointments they get. There are a few reasons for this. It shows efficacy but can also be used for motivation.

Consider making ten phone calls. Of those ten phone calls, let's assume that there are two rude people, four people who are not interested, and four people who will take a meeting. If this is the ratio then this means that if there are two rude people to begin with, then statistically, that is them out of the way for the rest of the ten calls.

The Magic Ratio

I was introduced to Pareto's principle early on in my career. The principle was established in 1906 by Italian economist, Vilfredo Pareto, after noticing that twenty per cent of the pea pods in his garden were responsible for eighty per cent of the peas. Pareto expanded this principle to macroeconomics and showed that eighty per cent of the wealth in Italy was owned by twenty per cent of the population. The principle states that eighty per cent of the consequences come from twenty per cent of the causes. In other words, eighty per cent of the results will come from twenty per cent of the effort.

In the 1940s, Dr Joseph Juran applied the 80/20 rule to quality control for business production. He showed that eighty per cent of product defects were caused by twenty per cent of the problems in production methods. By reducing the twenty per cent of production problems, overall quality could be improved. Further analysis has shown that:

- 80% of profits come from 20% of clients.
- 80% of total sales are generated by 20% of the sales reps.
- 80% of total profits are generated by 20% of customers.
- 80% of software crashes are caused by 20% of the most reported software bugs.
- 20% of patients account for 80% of healthcare spending.

The ratio is not always an exact 80/20 split. It could be 70/30, 95/5 or other combinations, but the point is to identify the imbalance and to focus accordingly. Juan sums it up nicely, "the vital few and the trivial many."

What Does This Mean for Business?

I was sceptical that this would be true for the industry that I was working in at the time. The company, which I worked for, was involved in selling life insurance products to intermediary Insurance Brokers. They, in turn, would recommend those products to their clients.

I decided to analyse my sales data and was very surprised to see that over 80% of business was coming from less than 20% of the brokerages. There was also a very long tail of small supporters. As I moved into Investment Management, the same principle also held true.

It is very tempting in sales to think that all we have to do is to get the long tail of low supporters to give us more business and we will achieve sales growth. However, the 80/20 principle says that this will not be the case. Often we can get more business from our key supporters together with upselling opportunities.

The principle also helps with difficult or problem clients. This is because we will get 80% of problems from 20% of our clients. I have known businesses that have got rid of problem clients because of the time involved in servicing them. It was becoming detrimental to the firm, and they cut them loose. By removing these clients it allowed the firm to focus on more profitable, and less time consuming clients. If one of the key clients represents one of the 20% of clients that are contributing to 80% of the revenue, then this has to be assessed and judged separately.

The 80/20 principle is a great guiding principle and experienced salespeople realise you can't appeal to everybody all of the time. One of the key sales skills is to narrow down the list of prospects and targets to a more manageable and profitable list.

CHAPTER 10

Preparing For Success

"You should never go to a meeting or make a telephone call without a clear idea of what you are trying to achieve."

Steve Jobs

Before looking at the skills and strategies, a key element of any sales process is preparation. Preparation is usually the part that most salespeople don't like. The fun part is getting out and about and seeing people.

DOING THE GROUNDWORK

Prospecting

It is worth spending time planning and identifying prospects to ensure that time is spent efficiently and not wasted. There are many ways to identify prospects. Industry data can be a good starting place, together with your company data and your knowledge. A method that works well is through networking. If you are already dealing with companies in a particular market, simply ask your customers which of their competitors they would rate. They will often give you information as to who to contact. Most times, they will be quite helpful and say, "Just mention that I said to give you a call."

Another method that works well is to get to know other salespeople. These are people that deal with the same firms that you want to get to know but that are supplying different products or services. This works particularly well if in a similar market, where you are not direct competitors. For example, imagine selling investment products to a financial advisor. If you are selling a product that invests in Japan, getting to know another salesperson that does not have a product that invests in Japan allows for the exchange of information.

An idea that works well when developing relationships with customers is to organise an event with another company that does not directly compete in your niche. The idea is to share the cost and promotional activity. The customer gets two offerings presented at once, which is more beneficial for them in terms of time.

An even more radical method is to organise an event with some of your direct competitors. Your competitors may have the same products or services that you offer, however, their offering may not be their strongest. In this scenario, they may be willing to forgo promoting in areas that overlap, to promote their stronger offering.

These approaches will depend on your industry. However, it is worth thinking outside the box, because as time becomes more constrained, hearing from two or three companies at once is far more efficient in terms of time for the customer.

Getting Past the Gatekeeper

When it's time to make the calls, it often works best to batch them together and to sit down and do a set number of calls in one go. The hardest one is the first call, so it makes sense to have in mind how many calls are in a batch that you are going to make and then take a rest.

A key skill to be honed is that of getting past the gatekeeper. Many businesses have a receptionist or a gatekeeper whose job is to screen telephone calls. If you are looking to arrange a meeting, getting past the gatekeeper to the decision maker is vital.

Large businesses operate within business hours and outwith these hours, the phones are not answered. Many smaller businesses, however, often answer the phone outwith business hours and the owner of the business or a senior member of staff will often take the call. If it is not possible to get through in business hours, try calling either first thing in the morning or later in the evening.

A good receptionist will be well trained to ask the right questions but many are not and this represents an opportunity. The first thing to do is to make sure that our mental state is correct. Before making the call, we must assume that we are going to get through and that it would be strange if the receptionist did not put us through.

People respond to authority and confidence. It is important that when speaking on the phone that you display confidence.

Preparing for Success

A good way to convey confidence is to make sure that when speaking that your tone goes down at the end of the sentence, as this is associated with a command. If you rise in tone at the end of the sentence, you need to be aware of this. An upward tone is associated with a question and will be interpreted as such at the unconscious level, and this does little to convey authority.

A method that is useful when phoning, is to ask for the person by their first name. This works well, particularly in a small business, where there is only one person there of that name. A lot of how we interpret our everyday world is based on presumption and assumption. By simply asking for a person by their first name conveys the impression that we know them. This works as long as your voice is congruent. The typical response is either one of two.

"Yes sure, or *one minute, I'll put you through."*

When we hear this, we are likely to be put through.

If we hear *"Who's calling?"*

then we know that there is a good chance that they are going to ask for more information.

This must be answered correctly and confidence displayed at this point. An effective way to display confidence is instead of saying,

"My name is...."

Substitute this with,

"This is....", and then your name.

A method that is useful when someone asks *"Who's calling?"* is to simply give your name and not your company name. I learnt this early in my sales career when struggling to get past receptionists. I remember being in an office waiting to meet with a customer and I heard one receptionist say to the other, "You know these salespeople are quite clever. They never mention the company that they work for!" From that moment on, I have used this and found it to be very effective. It works particularly well if it is the type of business where they deal with individual clients and they don't want to appear rude on the phone. They may mistake you as a client!

If you do feel that you want to give your company name in addition to your name, simply say, this is Bill Smith, Development Director, and then the name of your company. This works particularly well if you have a good title.

And Which Company Are You Calling From?

A trained receptionist will often ask, *"And which company are you calling from?"* If you have met the person before, a useful phrase is *"It's ok he knows who it is."* A word of caution here. Only use this phrase if you have met the person before and they are likely to remember you. Often a receptionist will say, *"Will he know what it is in connection with?"* A phrase that works very well is to use the word *"need"* rather than *"would like to."* It's always useful to put context around this request as well.

"I need to speak to David to discuss IT issues."

If they ask for more information, you could say,

> *"We've got this really clever system that we have found works exceptionally well with companies, just like yours, that I'm sure David would be interested in. It saves you time and money. I need just three minutes of his time and he can decide how he would like to proceed."*

Another phrase that you can use is,

"It's just a quick courtesy call," and then your reason.

If you can put some context around the reason for the call, this can make things easier. If you previously have met the person at a trade fair and they have asked you to give them a call sometime, then all you have to say is,

> *"I met David at the trade fair and he asked me to give him a call."*

An effective method is to send somebody a letter in advance. It is so unusual in these days of digital communication to send a letter that it creates a good impression and secondly, it allows you to say,

> *"I'm calling David following my recent letter."*

This sounds more important and will often enable you to be put through. As we deem letters to be more personal, it is unlikely that the receptionist will ask about the content.

Much of communication takes place at an unconscious level and it is not just the words, but it is the delivery and the correct manner that will ensure success. When speaking to the gatekeeper, try to be as vague as possible. *"Vaguely specific"* as I like to call it.

They Won't Call You Back

Unless you know the person, don't expect them to return your call and don't ask them to phone back. I have found that leaving a message and asking to return my call to be an unsuccessful approach. Early in my sales career, I joined a company and had a list of firms to contact. I was sitting next to a more experienced salesperson, and I began going through my customer list and phoning each customer one by one. I couldn't get through to any of them so I left a message for each of them to call me back. On completion, I sat back looking pleased with myself and the more experienced salesperson asked; *"What are you doing?"* I replied that I just phoned everyone on my customer list, and I was just waiting on them to call me back. A wry smile appeared on his face and, sure enough, none of them called me back.

If the receptionist says, *"Shall I ask him or her to call you back?"* saying, *"No"*, can sound a bit abrupt. I have found a method that works well is to say,

> *"It's OK, I am going to be on the phone myself and we will end up missing each other. I'll try again later. When is the best time to try?"*

A method to use, if unable to speak to the person after repeated attempts, is to say to the receptionist,

> *"I'm sorry to keep bothering you. Is there a direct dial number I could contact David on, or do you have a mobile number?"*

Often, they will not give these numbers out, but sometimes they do, and if you don't ask, you don't get.

He is in a Meeting

Many of us have had the experience of repeatedly calling and being told that the person is in a meeting. I have had that experience before many times and it can become incredibly frustrating. However, many people allow gatekeepers access to their diaries and to book meetings for them. Asking the question,

> "Does he keep his own diary?"

can save hours and hours of telephone tennis. Often, they will say, I have it in front of me. Sometimes the receptionist will say that they will have to check with the individual first. If this happens, all you have to say is,

> "That's great, I quite understand. Is it possible to pencil in Tuesday at 3:00 o'clock and if you'd be kind enough to confirm if that works, that would be fantastic?"

IT'S TIME TO SPEAK

Once You Have Been Put Through

Once you are put through, make sure to have the bullet points written down, or a mind map of the points to cover to help steer the conversation. A useful technique is to pace the person and describe what they must be feeling. For example,

> "I know you must get many people phoning up and wasting your time and I find it frustrating as well. The purpose of this call is not to waste your time but to very briefly and simply show you how we can save you time and money."

Remember when you first call someone, the recipient's brain is in a slight state of confusion. They are wondering why you are calling. The sooner you can reduce the level of confusion and provide some context, then the sooner this calms the reptilian brain. If you can put context around the call, this helps. Even if you have only met them briefly before, it's perfectly fine to say,

> "Hello John, it is Bill Smith. We met at a trade fair and you mentioned getting in touch with you."

This gives context to the call. Force yourself to raise your energy levels and to be cheerful without appearing false. Don't ask them how they are doing today as they don't know you and just want context as quickly as possible. Whatever you do, don't be mechanical and never read from a script!

What Is the Objective When You Get Put Through?

For many people, the purpose of the phone call is to arrange a meeting with the customer. When you are put through, you need to state your name, title, and company. You need to get to the point very quickly and to explain what's in it for them. Remember to do this confidently and with a tone that goes down at the end of the sentence. Someone's interest must be piqued without giving any details.

> "I want to talk to you about a unique way of handling digital marketing that you won't have seen before. If you are free for ten minutes, I would like to come and show you how this can increase sales and revenue for you and your business? When would be most convenient next week or the week after?

One of the biggest mistakes that people make when they are put through is to try to arrange a meeting with the customer immediately. The customer then asks *"What is it you want to meet about?"* The salesperson then starts to describe in great detail the product or service. The customer often replies now that they have heard what you had to say, there's no need to meet up. The way around this is to be artfully vague or "vaguely specific" as I prefer to say. Social proofing can be incorporated to help with this.

Social proofing is one of the biases that is hard-wired into humans and it is a useful one to incorporate when we first speak to the customer. We all prefer to use something that others have endorsed or liked. We could mention that we deal with many businesses, *just like theirs,* or that businesses, *just like theirs,* have shown the greatest interest in our new process. Another description is that our service is designed to streamline and make product distribution easier, more cost-effective and that it is being used extensively in businesses *just like theirs.* We then ask if they would be free for fifteen minutes, either next week or the week after, to enable us to show how this could benefit them and their business.

The customer will often then say, *"What exactly is it?"* An inexperienced salesperson will then describe all the features of the product or service that they have. Do not do this! Remember, at this stage, we are not trying to sell the offering, we are merely trying to arrange a meeting so that we can discuss the offering. We need to be vague, but appear to be specific. Think about this as a bit like peeling an onion. We don't want to go straight to the core, but to peel off layers one by one. Next, we want to be as vague as possible.

> *"It's very difficult to describe over the phone. It's a unique system that helps you to maximise your distribution and minimise your cost."*

Often at this stage, the customer's interests will have been piqued. They may, however, still come back and ask for more details about the offering. We now take off the second layer of the onion.

> *"This is a system that we have developed that is tried and tested and is used by many other companies, just like yours, to produce dramatic improvements in distribution while making significant cost savings. It is difficult to describe over the phone and it's much easier to show you face to face. When would you be free for ten minutes next week, or the following week, so that I can show you how this may be of benefit to you?"*

The customer may still come back and ask you to send something that they can look at. If they ask for this, most times, it is just a smokescreen. I have found it useful to say,

> *"Of course, I would be delighted to send you the information, but you know what it's like when we get large PDF documents sent through by email. We are all busy and it takes a while to read. If you have just 10 minutes free, I can run through it with you over a coffee, if that works better for you, and this saves you having to*

trawl through a 40-page pdf document, which nobody likes doing."

Being prepared is important because this is like a game of poker, where the last thing to do is to show your hand too early. Remember, this is a numbers game and it will not be possible to get a meeting with every single customer that you contact. If a customer says "No", don't worry. This is simply one of the customers that are not going to be part of your 80/20 list. Make a note of conversations as it allows the opportunity to revisit if things change and for common objections to be identified.

TIME TO TRAVEL

Planning the Territory

There are three aspects to planning the territory.
1. Targeting key prospects.
2. Servicing key customers.
3. Time management.

Targeting the Key Prospects

The first task is to identify and target the key customers and prospects and divide them into Tiers. Tier 1, Tier 2, etc. A useful method is to write down all the customers or clients that you want to make contact with on an A4 sheet of paper, a notebook or in an e format. Once contact is made with that customer or business, cross out the name on the list together with a note of the outcome. The following day, use the same list until all names are crossed from it.

Managing Your Time

Start by arranging meetings with key Tier 1 customers. Doing this allows the key customers to choose the times that are most convenient for them. Once those customers have been booked, it allows filling in the gaps in the day with customers that would be Tier 2 or Tier 3. When planning meetings it is easy to avoid customers who may appear challenging or ones where it is a struggle to arrange a meeting with and just opt for the easy ones.

When travelling, be as prepared and as organised as possible. Planning well ahead allows meetings in the same geographical area to be arranged, thus minimising travel time. With experience, you will work out the ideal duration of a meeting. For me, it was an hour, and it was like an inbuilt alarm that let me know that it was time to draw the meeting to a close. Often, a meeting is cancelled or is running ahead of schedule. Make use of this extra time to contact customers or clients and arrange meetings for the weeks ahead.

Some customers or clients respond to emails for meeting requests, while others ignore them. Developing a closer relationship with customers and clients allows other methods of communication, such as the use of text or social media. Remember, it's what suits the customer and not you. When arranging a meeting, make sure to give businesses plenty of warning and not ask to see them the following week.

When organising meetings, it makes sense to avoid travelling a long way for just one meeting. You may know of firms that are notorious for cancelling meetings at short notice. Always try to put these firms first thing in the morning, or last thing at the end of the day. This means that travel plans can be altered and this minimises gaps in the middle of the day.

When a customer or client agrees to a meeting, always confirm the time and location.

> *"Just to confirm, the meeting is at 10.00 o'clock on the 15th of May. Can I just check your address again?"*

It is surprising how many businesses move and the address is not updated. Some even have a different address listed, which may be their registered address.

When travelling, send a reminder email to the prospect or customer a few days ahead of travelling just to remind them of the meeting. There is nothing more annoying than being informed that the person is not in today or that they don't have it in the diary.

There is an exception to this, and that is where a meeting is with somebody likely to cancel at the last minute. Emailing in advance allows them to cancel. Simply turning up as agreed means that they will often see you. It is not a wise thing to do if travelling a long way for one meeting.

If kept waiting for a long time, don't allow yourself to be devalued. If the customer has not appeared after ten minutes, check with the receptionist how much longer they are going to be. If they are still in their previous meeting, ask the receptionist if they have their diary to hand and reschedule the meeting, explaining that you have other meetings to go to. Use your judgement when doing this. Often, the absent person will get in touch afterwards, apologise for not taking the meeting and next time they are more receptive.

CHAPTER 11

The Meet And Greet

"Everyone you will ever meet knows something you don't."

Bill Nye

Customs vary in different parts of the world and substitute what is acceptable in your particular culture. In most of Europe, the USA, Canada, New Zealand and Australia, the accepted greeting is the handshake. It is also important to smile before engaging in a handshake and to look somebody straight in the eyes. Remember, we are trying to stack as many things as possible in our favour.

DOING IT PROPERLY

The correct business handshake is to have your hand at right angles to the floor. In other words, extend your hand out in front of you with your knuckles on the right-hand side and your palm on the left-hand side. When shaking hands, make sure to have a firm grip. This does not mean the grip of a gorilla, nor does it mean a grip that is so weak that it feels like a wet fish. Accepted business etiquette is a firm handshake that is usually up and down about three times.

Amazingly, so few people are aware of the effect of a proper handshake. Many customers or clients have different types of handshakes and from this, you can gain some insight into their personality. It is worth practising the proper business handshake until it becomes automatic and you don't have to think about it.

Common Handshake Faults

1. Not gripping firmly enough.
2. Gripping too firmly to try and create authority.
3. A double-handed "glove" handshake often used by politicians to create warmth and trust.
4. A finger grab handshake. This is shaking the fingers rather than the hands.
5. The dominant handshake, where the arm is fully extended, with the knuckles facing upwards, and the palm facing downwards and thrust towards the individual.
6. Not looking at the person while you are shaking hands.

If you are meeting with colleagues in a group, make sure that when you shake the person's hand that you state your name and position within the firm or role within it. If meeting the person alone, then this is often accompanied by

"It's a pleasure to meet you" or "It's great to meet you."

Observe anything in your surroundings as this allows for small talk and to ask questions.

During the initial meeting, there is a lot of sizing up going on and you will be judged, just as you will be judging. It is important to control the frame and not to be seen to be subservient and just regarded as a salesperson. You are there to assist the person with a problem and to help them achieve their goals, or to make them feel better about themselves and their business. Your conduct, the way you look, move, speak, and act, will all convey whether you are a person that they wish to do business with and take seriously.

ENTERING THE ROOM

When entering the meeting room, it is advisable to ask where they would like you to sit, or to ask where the customer normally sits.

I remember going to visit a client with whom I had met many times previously. On this occasion, I was accompanied by some colleagues. The client had a lovely office with a large window with a beautiful view. I would often bring along experts from the firm and in return, they would organise a group meeting to discuss our offering. We would be shown into the room first and there was a large boardroom table in the centre of the room. Custom dictated that we would take the side of the table that was looking at, and out of the window, and our client would take their seats on the opposite side with their backs to the window.

On this particular occasion, we took the side of the table with our backs facing the window, which would normally be the client's side. It didn't register at the time that this was unusual. However, when they entered the room, they looked slightly confused and disorientated.

We are always trying to stack as much in our favour as possible and while this may only seem a minor point, these minor points can add up. People get surprisingly possessive about their chair, a spot in a park or the same locker in the gym.

From that moment on, whenever I enter another person's space, I always ask if they have a preference as to where they would like to sit.

Backs to the Wall

Many of us would not even think about which seat is best for a customer when selling or negotiating. If you are taking a client or customer out for lunch, or a coffee, always allow them to sit with their back to the wall. The back is the one area of the body that we cannot protect properly. People will unconsciously feel slightly on edge and their heart rate will rise if their back is exposed. In addition to this, always allow the client or customer to see where the exit point is. This was reinforced in a recent conversation with a client who admitted to always having to know where the exit is, or he feels uneasy.

A way to do this is to direct the customer and say, *"Why don't you have this seat?"* If you have a big deal that you wish to work on, book ahead at the restaurant and select a particular table. It is often worthwhile to get to know a restaurant so that you can have your "usual table."

These may seem minor points, but it is important to stack as much as we can in our favour. This is important when negotiating.

Small Talk

Once in the meeting room, it is normally accepted to have an element of small talk or preamble. It is difficult to give an exact duration for this as it varies with different individuals, industries, regions, and cultures. Learning to sharpen your awareness skills enables signs of discomfort to be spotted. Once this is detected, it means that the small talk is over. A sign that the small talk is over is that the sentences and the replies become shorter. Some people are keen to get straight down to business, whilst for others, getting to know people is a must.

Cornering It

I remember years ago when I was the manager of a life insurance company and had just been given a new office. The trend at the time was to move away from square to round tables to avoid the "them and us." This was seen as more conciliatory and less confrontational. If possible, when meeting with a customer, try to sit at right angles to the customer, and not directly opposite them. Awareness skills are important here. If somebody is sitting at a large desk and you suddenly spring up and sit at the side of their desk, this will not be appreciated and may be thought of as invasive.

A method to enable you to get around to the side of the desk is to show the customer or client a visual aid or chart. The way to do this is to say,

> "Would you mind if I sat around here, as it's easier to show you this chart as I'm not very good at reading upside down?"

CHAPTER 12

Asking The Right Questions

"Judge a man by his questions rather than by his answers."

Voltaire

We all experience reality differently and this is filtered through our five senses, which give us our unique view and interpretation of the world about us.

The only way to understand somebody else's map is to ask questions. This is one of the biggest areas where inexperienced salespeople make mistakes and yet is one of the easiest to correct. There are many types of questions that can be used. In this section, we will cover these in detail.

TIME TO ASK

Open Questions

Open questions are designed to elicit more information from the client or customer. These are questions that can't have a "yes" or "no" reply. Kipling said,

"I keep six honest serving men (they taught me all I knew); their names are. What, Why and When and How and Where and Who."

These words are powerful as they allow an exploration of someone's map to find out more information about them and their business. It is still possible to get short answers, but not the "Yes" or "No" response.

Example. *"How do you use open questions effectively?"*

One word of caution is when using the "why" question. The "why" question can make people quite defensive because you are questioning their judgement. It also causes them to justify their reasons for their actions and start reselling to themselves the very item that you are questioning.

Example. *"Why did you buy that car?"*

Closed Questions

Closed questions are questions where the answer is either yes or no. These questions are not good for eliciting information but are very useful in clarifying what somebody is saying. They are also useful if you want to narrow down the choices to either yes or no.

Example. *"Did you say that it was important to ask closed questions?"*

Rhetorical Questions.

Rhetorical questions are questions that do not require an answer and are often used by professional communicators, public speakers, and politicians. They are often used in the middle of a talk or if somebody is starting a speech. They allow you to ask a question that you want to provide an answer to.

Example. *"Now, why would we want to use rhetorical questions?" That is an excellent question and I'm going to explain to you why we need to use them."*

Tag Questions

Tag questions are questions that are often tagged on to the end of a statement to get a yes or no response. Positive tag questions are useful as part of the *"yes set",* which will be discussed at the end of this section. Tag questions include the phrases such as *isn't it, doesn't it, can't you, mustn't we and shouldn't you?*
Tag questions are useful because they can get people to say yes.

Example.

Even though you know I am using a tag question, it's very difficult to resist, isn't it?

Command Questions

Command questions are statements that sound like questions. They can be used very effectively to make the questioning sound more conversational. They are commands that are tagged on to questions.

Command questions are questions that often begin with *"Tell me," "Show me," "Explain to me," and "Let me understand." These* are often immediately followed by an open question.

Example. *"Tell me, what is it that excites you most about the business that you are in?"*

A word of caution when using command questions. When speaking, the emphasis is on the open question word, "what," and not on the words, "tell me." In the above example, the words, *"Tell me"* would be said fairly quickly, a short pause taken, and then the emphasis is placed on the second part of the sentence,

"What is it that excites you most about the business that you are in?"

The Yes Set

My preference in sales is to have a genuine desire to get to know the customer and to help them with their problem. I am less keen on methods that are just techniques and "salesy." That being said, there is a method that can be very effective both in building rapport and being more conversational. I would add a word of caution with this. If used sparingly, it can be very effective and if overdone, it can destroy any rapport that you may have built.

The technique is called the "yes set." It is a classic technique and the principle is that the more often you can get a customer to say *"yes,"* then the more likely they are to say yes to a sale. It

Asking the Right Questions

can be a great way to build up some rapport and to get the customer's mindset in a positive frame.

It is often started with a long statement type of question that is designed to elicit the yes response. This is then followed by another question and another question. For example.

"Would you say that choosing a company with a good reputation for providing quality products together with first class service is important?"

"Yes"

"Would it be fair to say that you would rather use a company with solid financials?"

"Yes"

In this example, the customer says yes twice. Unless this is done skilfully, it can come across as a bit clunky.

Yes Tags

A better way of doing this is to use positive tag questions. The key is to use these subtly, not overuse them and avoid being manipulative. Let's take the statement first.

"If you look at this chart, it shows just how strong the performance has been."

This is quite a dissociated statement, as the customer does not have to engage much. Making a simple change gets the "yes set" started.

"If you look at this chart, you can see just how strong the performance has been, can't you?" Or,

"Performance is important, isn't it? Have a look at how our investment has performed. It looks very strong, doesn't it?"

When using tag questions, people process information at an unconscious level. They will often respond by a nodding of the head or saying *"Yes"* without realising it.

Use this sparingly and always remember to have a desire to connect with the customer and to do the best for them. We don't want to come across as a manipulator. After all, we all want a win-win situation, *don't we?*

SOFTENING THINGS

Language softeners

Language softeners are phrases that can make questions seem more conversational and less intrusive. When finding out the information, we don't want to make it seem like an interrogation. Think about language softeners as wrapping paper. They dress the question up to make it seem more appealing.

Robert Cialdini discovered people are more predisposed to do something if given a reason. We can use this principle with language softeners. If I wanted to find out what somebody's biggest challenge is in their business, I could simply ask,

"What is the biggest challenge that you face in your business?"

There is nothing wrong with asking this question. The only issue is that it is quite direct and has little context. Ask too many of these types of questions and it becomes like an interrogation. Let's look at how we can soften this.

Asking the Right Questions

We all like context. Have you ever had a conversation with somebody and they start speaking randomly out of the blue? They assume that you know the context in which they are speaking about. It's quite annoying as we desperately try to make sense and put some context and meaning around what it is that they are saying.

A better way to ask questions is to use a language softener in front. This does two things

1. It puts context around your question.
2. It provides a reason for answering the question.

An example of this would be,

"<u>So that I can understand your business better</u>, what is the biggest challenge that you face in your business at the moment with product distribution."

Just presupposing

A way to soften this further is through the use of presuppositions. For the listener to make sense of the sentence, then part of the statement is presupposed and presumed to be true. It is easier to illustrate this with an example.

"<u>When you buy this product</u>, you may decide to upgrade"

In this sentence, it is presupposed that a purchase is going to take place. What is in question is whether or not an upgrade is going to take place.

Let's go back to our original example and this time we are going to add the phrase "would you be able to let me know."

So that I can understand your business better, *would you be able to let me know* what is the biggest challenge that you face with sales distribution currently?

In this statement, it is presupposed that the person will answer the question. The focus is on whether or not they will be able to let you know.

IT'S A QUESTION OF ASKING

The Interrogators

Interrogators ask one question after another without any reference or linking. In this case no comments are made and questions are just asked.

> *"Where do you invest?*
> *What type of funds do you buy?*
> *Who are you using?"*

Answerer and Questioners

"Answerers and Questioners" answer the question first and then turn it into a question. An example would be,

> *"Presumably you invest in the US and Europe using mutual funds, direct equities and bonds, would that be correct?"*

Question and Answerers

"Question and Answerers" are closely related to the above and are people that ask a question and then answer it themselves. An example is,

"What type of investments do you invest in? Is it bonds, hedge funds, mutual funds, equities that sort of thing?"

Question, "Yes and I"

"Question, Yes and I" ask a question and immediately, on hearing the answer, start talking about themselves. Let's look at an example.

Questioner

"Have you ever invested in US smaller companies?"

Customer

"Yes."

Questioner

"I have invested in US smaller companies in the past myself. I had a really good experience. In fact, the first time was back in the 90s and it was with a broker, a friend of mine that recommended that this was the market to be in."

The customer is likely to be uninterested in any of this information.

The Apologetic Questioner

Apologetic questioners lack confidence and apologise for asking a question. There is a difference between being polite and showing no authority or command of the conversation.

An example is,

> "If it's not too much trouble, I don't want to appear as if I'm asking anything out of turn and if you don't feel comfortable telling me this information, that's ok. Would it be possible, if you don't mind, to let me know a little bit about your business?"

The Interrupters

These are people who ask a question and then, before the answer is complete, interrupt and ask another question. Sometimes they may even interrupt to talk about themselves again.

If someone has asked you a question and doesn't let you answer, but interrupts, it is very annoying. A customer may put up with one or two interruptions, but if this is ongoing, it will start to annoy them. There are three exceptions where an interruption is acceptable.

1. If a term or an abbreviation is used which is one that you're not familiar with, or you are confused by. If, for example, the acronym BDF is used and you don't know what the BDF stands for, simply saying "BDF?" with a rising tone allows clarification without appearing intrusive.
2. If the customer keeps talking and goes on and on without a gap in speaking.
3. If the customer keeps going off on a tangent and there is a need to bring them back to the point.

Be very careful when interrupting as people don't like it. The best approach is to allow someone to finish and to minimise your interruptions.

CHAPTER 13

Detectives And Funnels

"Most people do not listen with the intent to understand; they listen with the intent to reply."

Stephen R. Covey

After the initial meet, greet and small talk, it's time to find out more about the customer's challenges or aspirations. Questioning aims to make sure that the product or service addresses a problem or provides a solution for the desired outcome.

THE SALES FUNNEL

The questioning process can be represented by a funnel with the wide part at the top and the narrow part at the bottom. This represents a great metaphor. Imagine that the customer has as a secret and, just like a detective, you have to find out what that is.

Detectives & Funnels

All Possible Outcomes

Questioning   Clarifying

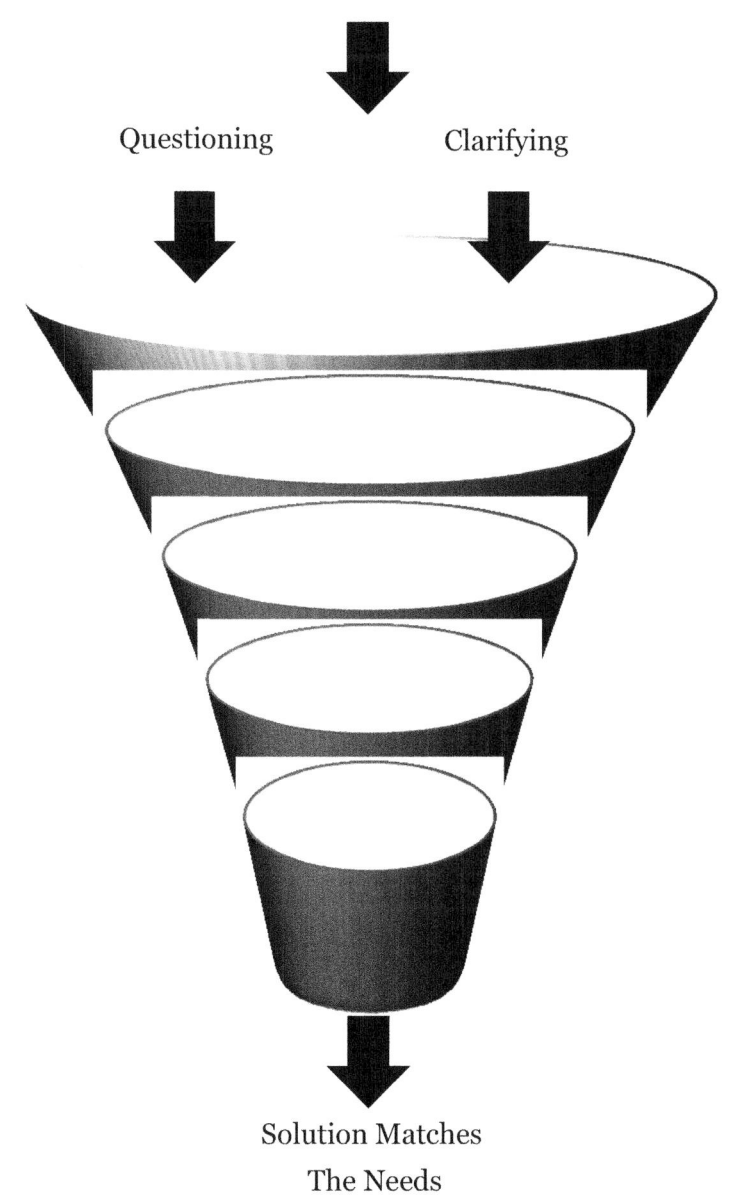

Solution Matches
The Needs

Fig.5

Imagine all the pieces of information at the top of the funnel. With questioning, this is narrowed down until only one piece of information will fit through the narrow part of the funnel. Moving down the funnel, the understanding needs to be periodically clarified. This is done by summarising the information and repeating it back to the customer or client.

It is easy to assume that we have heard something that we haven't. People often don't describe things clearly, which causes a misunderstanding. Repeating back periodically ensures clarity of what has been said and enables any misunderstandings to be corrected. At the end of the funnel, there should be a complete understanding and agreement of the solution, product or service that fits with the customer's needs.

Going Down the Funnel

The first step is the use of open questions to find out the problem or requirement. Let's look at selling mutual funds as an example.

A mutual fund is an investment product that holds a basket of different companies' shares and or bonds on behalf of an investor. This enables the investor to have small ownership of many companies, thereby spreading and reducing risk. Mutual funds each have a different investment objective and many invest in specific countries.

Let's assume we are meeting with a client and want to promote a mutual fund that invests only in US companies. The opening question may be.

"To make sure that we are only discussing areas that are of interest to you, I wonder if you be good enough to

outline the types of investment products that you use and recommend to your clients?"

The customer then responds and gives a full outline of all the product types they use. As part of that response, the customer mentions they use mutual funds. A closed question is then used to find out and narrow down to see if US funds are used. The next question.

"Do you use mutual funds that just invest in the US?"

Let's assume that the customer confirms this. We now have some information but are nowhere near the point of presenting. This is only the very beginning of the process. This is where many salespeople go wrong and start pitching their product far too soon. However, we don't have enough information to even begin to think about presenting. The next question is.

"That's great that you use mutual funds that invest in the US. I wonder if you would be able to outline the main criteria that you look for when selecting mutual funds that invest in the US."

At this point, the customer will list the criteria for selection. On receipt of this information, we are still not ready to start presenting. The next thing to do is to repeat back all the information to the customer.

"Just to check my understanding, the main criteria you look for when selecting a mutual fund that invests in the US is....."

The criteria are then listed back. The customer confirms that this is correct and the next question to ask is,

> *"Are there any other things that you look for when selecting a mutual fund that invests in the US?"*

At this point, the customer will often add something else to the list. We then repeat the list back again with the full criteria and at the end say,

> *"So, there is nothing else that would be a consideration when selecting a mutual fund that invests in the US?"*

During the questioning process and while the customer is listing all the criteria, make sure to go through a mental checklist of the criteria and the degree to which your product or service matches the criteria that the customer has listed. If it is found that the product fails on one or two of the criteria, then it needs to be established whether these criteria are essential, or whether they are a nice to have. The customer's full criteria for purchase having been established, it's time to move to the next stage.

Checking Out the Competition

At some point, the customer's current supplier is going to have to be established. It is at this point that many salespeople make a big mistake. As soon as the competition is mentioned, they want to immediately inform the customer why their product or service is much better. This is completely the wrong thing to do and should be resisted at all costs. To explain why, we must understand how people think.

Pushing & Pulling

As discussed earlier, if I push or pull you, there would be a natural resistance. Resistance is not just physical resistance.

People will always resist what they are told and accept what they conclude. There is an exception to this and that is most people are hard-wired to have a deference to a higher authority. This means that they are more likely to accept suggestions from people in authority or an expert.

It's Getting Heated

Have you ever been involved in an argument or a debate where you had a view that was in opposition to the viewpoint of another person? It may have been a minor disagreement to begin with. Then, as the discussion continued, the other person started to force their opinions upon you. Even though initially you didn't feel that strongly about the issue, the very fact that someone is forcing their opinions makes you want to resist what they are saying. If this carries on, then more resistance occurs and you end up defending a viewpoint that initially was not that important.

What is happening here? When someone challenges someone else's opinions or thoughts, we are witnessing a challenge to somebody's criteria and values. Each one of us has our opinions and thoughts, based on our own criteria and values, which have been established throughout our life. We filter our reality through our five senses and form a map of the world. We use this to form our decision. People will naturally resist what you tell them, particularly if you try to force them. People rarely like to be told what to do. The more that you force them, just as in the imaginary example where I was pushing or pulling, the more that they will resist.

Compliment the Decision

Something that works very well is to compliment someone on their choice of supplier, product, or service. This gives credit for the decision making process and calms the reptilian brain. For example,

"ABC is a fantastic company, and they have got some amazing products."

This allows the customer to feel that their decision making has been respected. Having done some preparation, you should know something about your competitors. We now have to tread carefully when introducing our product or service.

Final Probe

There is still a bit more information to find out first before we get to the presentation of a product or service. Having complimented the customer on their choice of supplier, the last thing we want to do is to ask why they like them. You may remember from the section on questions the importance of being careful with the question "why." The reason for this is, for them to answer the question, they have to think about the reasons as to why they are using that particular company. This results in a process called revivification, as they relive the selection process used to select from that company in the first place. They then start reselling the offering to themselves.

Instead, subtly ask, is there anything that is missing from the current product or service that you're using? Watch and observe the customer. They may struggle to think of something and may need some prompting. Knowing that you are cheaper than your competitor, you could ask how happy they are with the price they are paying, or if you know service levels are an issue, then service levels can be explored.

Another area to explore is to ask about something that your competitor does not have, that you do. Let's just suppose that your company has an app that makes it easy to place orders and provides data while they are away from the office. You also know that the competitor does not offer this. Asking innocently about their experience with the competitor's app causes the customer to mention that there is no app and we can explore this.

Sometimes the customer will say that they are very happy with their current supplier and that there are no issues or improvements that they are looking for. If this happens, then there is only one strategy left to try. For this to be effective, knowledge of your industry and your competitors is a must. The aim here is to show how your product or service can sit alongside their current choice to enhance what they currently offer. They may consider incorporating your offering and allocate some budget to your company. This type of sale can be very effective, particularly if you have done your research.

The types of situations where this type of approach would work are:

1. Where it can be shown that exposure to just one provider adds risk.

2. Using a niche product that can establish the relationship before targeting the larger area of business.

3. Showing them that by incorporating your product and service, alongside the products and services that they currently use, will provide their customers with a better experience.

Remember, it's better to get some support than none at all.

LEARNING TO LISTEN

Two Ears and One Mouth

It has been said that we have two ears and one mouth and that they should be used in that order. It is an old cliché, but worth remembering. Our senses are being bombarded by data all the time. Our brain can't process all the information at the same time. This means that sometimes we don't hear everything. If we are thinking about what to say next, then we cannot be listening properly. Listening skills and questioning techniques are at the heart of excellent sales skills together with belief, state control, rapport, and awareness (BSRA). There are two parts to listening skills.

1. Listen to what the customer is saying.
2. Look like we are listening to what the customer is saying.

I remember being asked to be a judge for a sales competition at Napier University in Edinburgh, Scotland. I observed that some of the competitors were not asking the right questions and some were not listening properly to the answers. There was an inward focus, as if thinking about what to say next.

Active Listening

A technique that you can use is to repeat with your internal voice exactly what the customer is saying to you. This requires that you pay attention. It can be quite tiring and requires practice, but develops the habit of active listening. It is important to appear to listen too.

How to Look Like We Are Listening

Three things convey listening. The first of which is eye contact and looking at someone without staring. Some find looking into somebody's eyes uncomfortable. Something that makes this easier to do is to pick a spot between the eyes and look at that instead. This is close enough to appear to look into their eyes without creating that uncomfortable feeling. It is important not to eyeball the customer. Remember to periodically move the gaze away from the spot.

A useful way to show that you are listening is to tilt your head slightly to one side. This does not mean tilting at 45 degrees but just a slight head tilt at about 20 degrees off vertical is suffice. Head tilting is an unconscious response to listening and will be read as such. Periodically nod your head in agreement. This happens naturally and unconsciously and will be read as listening and agreeing.

CHAPTER 14

It's Time To Present

"They may forget what you said but they will never forget how you made them feel."

Carl W. Buehner

The moment has now arrived, and it's time to present the solution. Before starting, it is vital to be seen as credible.

BEING CREDIBLE

A way to establish credibility is to admit to a small weakness in the offering initially. People are naturally suspicious and expect someone to say how wonderful their product or service is. Their guard will be up because they expect it.

Imagine meeting for the first time and I said that I was good at skiing, football, tennis, rock climbing, cycling and swimming. Assuming that these are all true, which they are not, by the time that I had got past football and tennis, your suspicions may have become aroused and you may think that it's unlikely that I would be good at all these things. This creates doubt in your mind and negates the possibility that I may be good at skiing and good at football. If, on the other hand, I admit to not being particularly good at swimming, but that my real strengths are skiing and football, you are more likely to accept that I may well be good at those.

There is a dilemma at play here. How can we create credibility but also admit to some form of weakness? There is a way to do this. Let's look at an example of selling a mutual fund that invests in US smaller companies to a financial advisor. The first statement establishes credibility.

> *"We are an award winning Investment Management firm. We specialise in investing in US companies."*

Having established credibility and context, it's time to create some trust by admitting to a small irrelevant weakness.

> *"We don't pretend to be all things to all men. We do have other investment products, but I wouldn't feel comfortable recommending some of them to you, as I don't think that they are our strongest offerings. However, one of our strongest offerings is the fund that invests in US smaller companies.*

It is important to be truthful with your customers. Credibility and trust are like virginity; you only lose them once.

THE REAL SECRETS

Let's now start getting into the content. Beware of product vomit. I learnt this phrase from one of my early training courses involving intermediary sales. I think it sums up this mistake well.

Many salespeople get so excited at the opportunity to promote their product and service that they feel this compelling need to get every feature about their product out of their mouth as quickly as possible. This is dumped onto the customer without conveying any benefits. A feature is just that and it does not convey any benefits to the customer. It is a statement. The customer does not have to imagine or contextualise anything.

A Magic Phrase

There is a simple way to turn features into benefits and I learnt this at one of my first sales courses over thirty years ago. It's a wonderful little phrase which is, "which means that." This phrase is so useful that it can be used on a one to one and group basis. It involves, whenever a feature of our product or service is stated, simply tagging on the phrase, "which means that."

Let's look at an example and imagine describing a feature of a car which is "four wheel drive." This is a feature and is just a statement. Let's add the aforementioned phrase. This car has four wheel drive, which means that, if the road surface is covered with snow and is slippery, it provides much greater grip. "Which means that", conveys the benefit. When we say the phrase, "which means that", and then describe the car being in the snow and on a slippery surface, then the customer has to imagine it to make sense of it. The customer is therefore far more engaged. If this can be linked to someone's criteria and values so much the better, let's suppose it is "family safety". This car has four wheel drive, which means that if the road surface is covered with snow and is slippery, it provides much greater grip, which means that you and your family will be safer.

There is another reason that this phrase is so useful. If presenting to somebody, it enables a level of knowledge to be displayed and explained without it coming across as patronising, *"which means that"* you will be a better communicator, doesn't it?

The Secret Sauce

To maximise the impact of the features and benefits principle, the more of the customers' senses that are engaged, the more they are going to identify with the benefit associated with that feature. Something that is vividly imagined and experienced uses the same parts of the brain for processing. For most products and services, this will be visual and feeling descriptions, but if the product has a unique sound to it, or smell to it, then this can be incorporated as well. It may be that the product is all about the taste, however, there will be other components to the experience as well.

Think about a car. How does it look, smell, sound, and feel to drive? How does it make you feel? How does it make others see you and how does it affect the way you see yourself? The more that we can create a detailed internal map for the customer, the more that they are going to engage.

WORD POWER

The Power of Words

When hearing a word, we have to process it first to discount it. For example, *"Whatever you do, don't think about a pink elephant."* First, we have to think about the pink elephant and then delete it.

The brain doesn't do negative language. First, it interprets something and then deletes it. Much of this occurs at an unconscious level and it gives important clues to help describe something to somebody. It is better to communicate with positive language than negative.

"Hold on tight!" is better than, *"Don't let go!"*

Language is incredibly powerful and it is how we suggest things. It is how we convey reality. Notice the effect of the sentence below.

"As you sit there, looking at this book, reading these words, really focus on these words. And as you carry on reading them and notice all the letters, the more you try not to think about it, the more that you'll notice the increasing feeling of wanting to SCRATCH."

Choose language with care. Changing words can make your description more colourful. For example, instead of saying,

"As we walked down the road." this can be substituted with

"As we ambled down the road."

The word "ambled" paints a different picture. Try to use more descriptive language when describing things, to create a more vivid experience. It is better to use words that have positive connotations.

"How much are you looking to pay?" feels different than,

"How much are you looking to invest?"

"When you invest in the solution," feels better than

"When you buy the product."

STORYTIME

I Want to Tell You a Story

I worked for a mutual fund investment company, a long time ago, and a large part of my job was as a presenter. I would be on my feet presenting mutual funds in front of groups of financial advisors in different parts of the country. Mutual fund presentations at that time were renowned for being overly complicated and incorporated lots of data. Even the best presenters struggled to get the audience stimulated, particularly when the material was heavy going, and often difficult to understand.

Imagine the scene, a large hotel room, the type that is used for small conferences with fifty middle-aged financial advisors, mostly men in attendance. The seats were set up theatre style and the temperature in the room was slightly warmer than comfortable. After the introduction and welcome, the objective of the presentation was outlined. Now it was challenging delivering a set presentation designed by someone else. After a while, some people in the audience started to get just a bit too comfortable and were on the verge of drifting off.

I knew that I was a competent presenter from the hundreds of positive feedback forms that I had received. It troubled me that some people were drifting off. I began contemplating this and realised that the most interesting and charismatic people were the ones that had great stories to tell. I wondered whether I could incorporate stories too. Feeling apprehensive, I waited for my next presentation. During my next presentation, I noticed that the interest of the audience was starting to fade. At that moment, I decided to introduce a story. It was almost magical. The moment that I started using the magic words, "I want to tell you a story", and began telling a story, something magical happened. Everybody's head lifted and I had their full attention. At this point, I didn't have the scientific research behind storytelling and its effectiveness, but I knew that the more a story and a metaphor were incorporated, the greater the ability to hold someone's attention. Little did I know that I had discovered what is known as a pattern interrupt, which is a break in the brain's predicted patterns.

A Friendly Chat

Think about meeting up with friends. We don't start relaying a series of facts. For example, imagine that we met and I started telling you that Mount Everest is 8,850 metres (29,035 feet) above sea level. I then continue to inform you that Edinburgh in Scotland has an average of 28.7 inches (730 mm) of annual rainfall and that California has an average temperature of 15.2 C (59.4 F). You would become bored fairly quickly. This is

It's Time to Present

because the imagination is not required to understand these facts. People don't communicate in this manner when they meet up. We communicate in stories and share experiences. These stories can be stories that relate to our personal life, work, or something interesting that has happened to us.

We are hard-wired to listen to stories, and the latest research has shown that when a story is told, the brains of the storyteller and the listener synchronise. Jonas Kaplan, assistant professor of psychology at USC Dornsife, explains that one of the biggest mysteries of neuroscience is how meaning is created out of the world. Stories are a fundamental part of this and help create this meaning.

Playing the Part

The only way to understand a story is to imagine and play a part in that story yourself. To make the story more powerful, make sure that the story that you are using is as relevant to an experience that people can relate to. When using stories, avoid being too niche. For example, if using a weightlifting story to illustrate a point, the vast majority of people will not identify with the story. The story, its context, and the characters must be something that the other person can identify with.

Good communicators and salespeople have a file of good stories that can be used repeatedly to illustrate different points. Keep a record of good stories and it is worthwhile practising storytelling. We all know people who are bad storytellers. For example,

> "I was in Edinburgh last Monday, or was it Tuesday? Let me see, it must have been the Monday because I was at the

doctor's before, and I then drove into town about 11 a.m. or was it 11.15 a.m." The detail is irrelevant. It is the message that people are looking for.

PATTERN INTERRUPTS

Doing Something Different

People have limited attention spans. In the first five to ten minutes, they will be curious about you and what you have to say as they try to work you out. After this initial interest, the attention span drops as people tune out and go into their own internal world. They may wonder about what they are going to be doing at the weekend, a football game perhaps, or a party that they are going to. At this point, a pattern interrupt is required. This disrupts the brain's prediction of what will happen. It's a bit like when a loud noise frightens you and brings you back to the here and now. The environment has changed and with it our attention.

For a pattern interrupt to work, something different and unexpected is needed to get the attention back. Stories are pattern interrupts. Another pattern interrupt that works well is asking questions and using visual aids. Shock can also act as a pattern interrupt. I heard a story about a financial adviser, years ago, who, when selling life insurance, had a powerful method to reframe the importance of it for a family. The husband was the breadwinner and dealt with the finances. When sitting with a husband and wife, he would say,

"Tragically, your husband has been killed in a road accident."

"What happens now with the children?"

The husband would then say,

"We need to speak to your sister to....."

The adviser would then say.

"I am sorry, we can't hear you because you are no longer with us."

This is not an approach that everyone would be comfortable with but the story shows the power of a shock to get people thinking.

Everybody Loves a Mystery

I have attended many presentations over my career and I struggle to remember many of them. One presentation, however, stood out and I can still remember some of the content which was nearly 20 years ago. It was an economics presentation. I even remember the presenter's name, Bell, forecasting the price of oil at $30 a barrel.

Why was this presentation so memorable? The reason for this was that Bell had placed an acoustic guitar on the right-hand side of the stage as we looked at it. As soon as everyone entered the room, we all noticed the guitar immediately. The presenter had unwittingly created a mystery. People began wondering why is there a guitar on the stage. Is it going to be played and if so when? Every so often, Bell would move to the right-hand side of the stage near the guitar. Whenever he did so everyone wondered, "Is he going to play it now?" This happened several times during the presentation.

At the end of the presentation, he thanked everyone for coming and left the stage. We then left, having listened intently, hoping to get to the bottom of the mystery guitar. I still don't know to this day why the guitar was there, but it created a memorable and different event. There is a lesson to be learnt from this. If a mystery can be incorporated into a presentation, then this has the effect of increasing the listener's attention span. We can see this in marketing material where people will say, "If you watch this video to the end, I will share with you the biggest secret." Any form of mystery that you can create or incorporate will gain people's attention.

Not too Outrageous

Whenever presenting, whether on a one to one basis or in front of a group, we need to be different enough to be remembered, but not too outrageous that we are not taken seriously.

This explains why people will dress slightly differently. Perhaps, if you're a man, you may wear a bow tie, or a waistcoat (vest). If you are a woman, then you may have a particular colour or look associated with you.

We are used to seeing people dressed in a particular way and this creates their image and expected look. When we see them dressed differently, it somehow seems to alter our perception of them. Image is important. If it looks good, it is perceived as good.

COMFORT IN NUMBERS

Providing Comfort in Numbers

Most people don't like being the first to try something new, particularly if they have to pay for it. It is reassuring to know that other people have tried, done and found something useful and enjoyed it.

I had a summer job when I was a student. I worked at the local car dealership that sold Nissan cars. The dealership also had a franchise for Hyundai cars. Back in the late 1980s, Hyundai was an unknown brand. The cars were cheaper than the equivalent Nissan and you got a lot more car for your money. However, at that time, whenever trying to persuade someone to buy a Hyundai car over a Nissan, there was a natural reluctance. This was because people hadn't heard of Hyundai, which is hard to believe in today's terms. Customers were looking for reassurance that others had bought the Hyundai car and that it was reliable and of good quality.

This is what we call social proofing. It's the reason when shopping online that the first thing many of us look for is a review. I saw items listed on a large distribution platform that were identical. They had both been manufactured in China, and one had a logo on it and the other didn't. One had a nice photograph, with a 360-degree view, that had been digitally enhanced. The other product used a photograph taken on a kitchen worktop. The other big difference that I didn't mention was that the product with the logo and the nice photos had thousands of reviews, and yet was almost double the price of the cheaper one with hardly any reviews. When presented with those two products, most people will select the more expensive one, largely because of the number of positive reviews.

The same thing happens on social media. The more "likes" a piece of content has, then the more likely it is to be viewed. When looking at this in the context of a sales presentation, the more social proofing that can be included, the better. This can come from other people, firms, and influencers. If they are well known names, so much the better.

MAKING YOUR PRESENTATION CREDIBLE

Most salespeople will have some form of a sales presentation or supporting sales material. Please bear in mind though, that your customer is going to have their "BS" antenna on red alert. After all, it is likely that they are going to be shown information, performance data or a survey that shows the product or service in a positive light.

A way to add credibility to a presentation is to incorporate some independent articles that show the product or service positively. Testimonials from real and respected sources offer great weighting to a product or service. Remember to use these sparingly, as we are not trying to force the customer or client into something. We merely want to give some form of social proofing and allow them to come to the conclusion themselves.

When delivering the presentation, incorporate a credibility statement to begin with, then a small sign of weakness to gain trust. Place the most important messages at the beginning of the presentation and at the end. People will remember their first day at school or college and their last. Remember to use tag

It's Time to Present

questions, stories, and metaphors when going through the presentation. Metaphors are very useful as they can paint a picture.

Let's consider talking about investing in the stock market, which, as we all know, can be volatile. Let's assume that the investment product is a low volatile offering. Simply stating this does not convey a picture to the customer.

It is better if a short story or metaphor can be used. First, make the statement that stock markets can be volatile. Then discuss a less volatile investment that has proved very popular with many customers and clients in a story format. Let's use an example of this.

Imagine sailing at sea. Just like the stock market, the sea can be unpredictable, sometimes flat calm and at other times very rough. Some people enjoy the excitement and the challenge of a rough sea. Others prefer the predictability and reassurance of a calm sea. An investment strategy can be explained in these terms. Our investment offering is a low volatile investment and is a bit like going sailing in a calm sea. You won't experience the excitement of the highs and lows of a turbulent sea, but equally, you won't get seasick with worry.

Picture This

When presenting a solution, we want to engage as many of the customers' senses as possible. As a large part of the brain is responsible for processing images, pictures or diagrams should be incorporated into the presentation. A picture says more than a thousand words and whenever using a pitch book or a

Inside the Mind of Sales

presentation, it should contain pictures in place of words, to emphasise points and minimise text.

Always use only bullet points and minimise the text wherever possible. If using charts or tables, make them simple. It is far better to have three simple graphs than one graph incorporating too much data. If we detect that the customer or client is switching off, then simply hand them something to look at.

Never give a customer or client a brochure, presentation or pitch book at the beginning of the meeting, because if they open and start flicking through it, they will not be listening to you.

Stacking the Seesaw

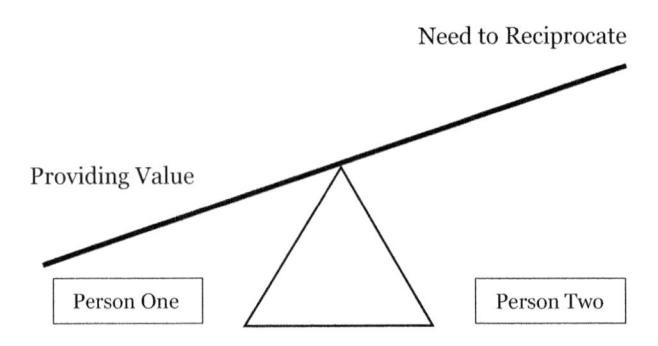

Fig.6

The law of reciprocity is a hard-wired behavioural bias. In short, this means that, if somebody does something for us, we usually like to return the favour.

If you've ever been invited around for dinner by some friends, you may casually mention that they must come round to yours next time. However, let's assume, before you get a chance to invite them around, they invite you around for lunch. Now, at this point, you realise that they've invited you twice and you haven't reciprocated. The seesaw is out of balance and it starts to feel uncomfortable. Your friends then invite you around for drinks. You either decline because you feel too embarrassed or insist on them coming around to yours. There will be some people who will take advantage, but for most of us, we want to make sure that the seesaw goes to level again.

We can use this in our sales approach. If we're providing the customer with great service and lots of value, this is seen as tipping the seesaw and they will want to reciprocate. Where most people go wrong is that they focus only on where they can help a customer in their business life. Imagine having met a customer and found out that they were a passionate food lover. Simply sending them an email after your meeting saying,

> *"I remember at our meeting that you mentioned that you are a lover of food. And I know of a great restaurant that is opening up in the area. I have a voucher for a free bottle of wine and have attached the voucher and thought that it might be of interest to you."*

This will work wonders. Corporate entertainment works similarly but has been reduced in many countries in recent years, due to some of the historical excesses. Done wisely, it still enables people to get to know each other.

Scarcity

The scarcity principle has been used extensively in sales and marketing. Direct marketers use this and sometimes there is a clock countdown on some of the web or funnel pages. The scarcity principle works because we don't want to miss out on something, and also, we want what we can't have. Scarcity is often used by car salesmen. The customer may well say,

> *"I'd like to think about it."*

The car salesman will then reply.

> *"That's great that you want to think about it, but I can't guarantee that this car is going to be here when you come back. We have had a lot of interest in it and there's a high probability that I will sell it."*

There is a dilemma. We want time to think about it and not rush into something but, equally; we don't want to miss out.

A way to imply scarcity is to mention that your company can't work with everyone, for example,

> *"We can't work with every firm out there. There are capacity limits as to how many firms that we can work with. We are nearly at full capacity and have identified your firm as an ideal firm to work with. I would hate for you to miss out on this opportunity.*

The scarcity principle can come across as slightly manipulative, but the reason that people use it is because it works.

Death by Pitch Book

Sometimes, a presentation can be quite technical and it's often accompanied by a pitch book. My experience of pitch books is that they have often been put together by people who've never been involved in meetings with customers and never presented a solution. Many lack a story, are far too complicated and have no obvious hook (what is in it for the customer).

One of the worst examples of a pitch book presentation I have seen was when I had a product specialist accompanying me on a client visit. The pitch book was opened on page one and the presentation composed of going through the whole presentation page by page. It was heavy going and needless to say, the client didn't invest with us.

One of the best examples of using the pitch book properly was used by a former colleague. My colleague asked the customer what they would like to cover. They just dipped in and out of the book, picking the relevant supporting graphics to illustrate the points. The individual also referenced academic research and used plenty of stories to illustrate the points.

The pitch book should be an aid to the presentation and not be the presentation. If there are any visual aids within the pitch book, the charts and graphs should be easy enough for a customer to understand. I have lost count of the number of visual aids that are so complicated that no one understood them.

Remember, get your hook message in early and address what's in it for them.

KISS

I learnt the acronym, KISS, early in my sales career when it was drummed into me, pardon the pun. KISS stands for "Keep It Simple Stupid." This is a great way to remember to keep things simple. If the information that you are conveying is too complicated and the customer is confused, they are likely to shut off. This will result in them deciding that what you are saying is not worth listening to.

Remember, the confused mind always says no and the suspicious mind always says no. A good test for your presentation is the "Gran test." If the concept or idea is too complicated for your Gran to understand, then it may need revisiting.

They Won't Remember

I want to share a story to illustrate just how little people remember what has been said.

I was once at an event with a previous company that I worked for. We were one of twelve companies presenting over two days. Each of the companies presenting had their own designated room to present from. Delegates from the conference would attend a selection of ten presentations over two days, by moving from room to room. Each presentation lasted around forty five minutes and there was a break to allow for movement and coffee.

After the event, I contacted each one of the delegates that had attended our presentation. Feedback was sought and their thoughts gauged. As I was working my way through the delegate list, there was one delegate that I was unable to speak to. He had gone on holiday for a week. I put it in my diary to contact him on his return, a week later. When I finally spoke to him and asked him what he thought of our presentation. His reply startled me.

"Was I at your presentation?"

It amazed me that he could not remember being there as our presenter was very good. However, just thinking about this

It's Time to Present

made me realise just how poor human recall is. I suppose that this is understandable if comparing to other situations.

Imagine watching a sports game or a soap opera on TV last night. If I asked what had happened during the game or the TV show you could probably recall fairly accurately, the events of the evening before. However, if I asked again a week later, recall becomes a little hazier. If I asked the same question a month from now, it would be a struggle to remember anything. Fast forward six months and you would be unlikely to recall any events at all. There is an exception to this and that is if something momentous, or memorable, had happened that could cement the memory.

If people choose to watch something that they enjoy and struggle to remember what has happened, what chance is there that they will remember something that is associated with work? If not convinced by this, the next time somebody attends a workshop or presentation, leave it a few days, and then ask them what they thought of the workshop or presentation. The reply is often that they enjoyed it and found it worthwhile. Then ask them which bits of the workshop or presentation they enjoyed the most. Notice how their recollection becomes vaguer. The longer you leave the point of contact, the vaguer their recollection becomes. You can have fun with this.

I have long held the view that the purpose of a presentation is not just to convey information. This may seem strange at first. I believe that the purpose of a presentation is to convey information so that the customer thinks, that is interesting I need to find out more. Knowing how short the human attention span is and the limits on recall, we must tie into the principle that "they may forget what we said, but never how it made them feel." For more advanced verbal communication methods, the reader is referred to HOW TO TALK TO ANYBODY by the author.

CHAPTER 15

Non Verbal Cues

"You see, but you do not observe."

Sherlock Holmes

I have been on training courses before where the trainer said, "If you had said this you would have closed the sale!" I remember thinking that this was a ridiculous thing to say. Human communication is far more than just putting the right words together.

COMMUNICATION MACHINES

What does "some" body mean

Communication among human beings is complex. It has been estimated that over 60% of how we communicate is carried out nonverbally. There have been different estimates from different sources. It's not important what the exact figure is. The key point is that nonverbal communication takes place, and it is important to recognise and interpret it. We can recognise someone who is in a bad mood without them saying anything. Here, the body language, demeanour and facial expressions all would indicate to tread carefully.

When communicating, it is important to be as congruent as possible, in other words, to make sure that the actions match the words. Most of us will have had the experience of listening to somebody and somehow it just didn't feel quite right. This is because signals are being picked up unconsciously, outside of our awareness, and are giving conflicting meanings.

Human beings are communication machines. We can't not communicate. The act of not communicating is an act of communication. This takes place at many levels and yet there is so much focus placed on what is said. Many are oblivious to the unconscious communication that is taking place. When reading body language, or nonverbal communication, it is important to look at clusters of behaviour and not isolated gestures.

The Limbic System

The limbic system is the part of the brain that reacts to the world around us automatically and instantaneously. It operates full time and is our emotional centre. From the limbic system, signals then pass to other parts of the brain. The limbic system creates an emotional response, which results in behaviours associated with survival instincts.

Survival mechanisms are hard-wired into the nervous system, making them difficult to disguise. For example, when we get a fright or are startled by a loud noise, these reactions occur unconsciously and are genuine. The limbic system is the part of the brain responsible for the fight, flight or freeze response and is considered our "honest brain."

The Neocortex or Critical Brain

This is the part of the brain that makes us different from other mammals. The neocortex analyses, evaluates, and critiques. It is the least honest part and is our "lying brain." It is the part of the brain that can deceive and it does so often. Yet, this is the part of the brain that we target and listen to for understanding.

Reading Nonverbal Communication

Research has established that people who can effectively read and interpret nonverbal communication and manage how others perceive them enjoy greater success in life than those who can't. Reading people successfully is a skill that comes with practice and becomes second nature. When learning a new skill, like driving a car, or a new sport, it might have felt overwhelming to begin with. However, after time and with practice, it becomes automatic.

People often ask if I am aware of everything that is going on with somebody's body language. For me, what happens is that something is suddenly raised to consciousness. For example, I was recently speaking to someone with whom I struggled with in the past. We were never on the same wavelength but recently had been getting on a lot better. When we were in dialogue, I was suddenly aware that our body language was in sync. This is a sign of rapport and being of like minds.

The problem is that most people spend their lives looking but not truly seeing. It is possible to go into great detail about body language and overly complicate things. A simple method is needed.

Two useful observations are to notice if somebody is in a position of comfort, or discomfort, and are they moving towards, or are they moving away from us? When we experience a sense of comfort, the limbic system "leaks" this information in the form of body language, which is congruent with our feelings. Observe someone relaxing by a beach and notice how their body reflects the state of comfort. The limbic brain experiences this and reflects this with nonverbal signals. Just watch anyone at the airport when a flight is cancelled or delayed and their body language says it all.

Movement

We move towards things that we like and move away from things that we don't. Think about two people that don't get on. They rarely sit next to each other in meetings and are usually as far apart as possible. If you tell someone that you want to share a secret with them, they will lean towards you to hear the secret.

Consider two people that are in rapport. When observing them, their body language will be a mirror image of each other and synchronised with each other. If we are speaking to somebody and we are in agreement, our body language will reflect this. If something is said that somebody doesn't like, the synchronisation breaks down and movement occurs. This results in a change in body language position and the "dance has been broken." This is something to be aware of.

The Clues

Body language can be very complicated, so let's look at some of the obvious things that give clues as to what somebody is thinking. We looked earlier at the importance of movement and establishing a position of comfort or discomfort. Let's look at some of the more obvious gestures that can give some insight.

HEAR, SEE AND SPEAK NO EVIL

"See No Evil"

Let's look first at the eyes. We look at things we like and look away from things that we don't. You may have heard people say, "I just couldn't even bear to look at her!" or "I just couldn't look!" Covering of the eyes is an obvious gesture and seen amongst young children. As we get older, the signals become more subtle and we learn to cover things up. Look for a change in blink rate, pulling at the eyelids, a reluctance to engage in eye contact or looking away.

"Hear No Evil"

Think of young children. When they don't want to hear something, they will cover both ears with their hands. In adulthood, we learn to be more subtle and is seen as tugging at the earlobe or playing with the ears. This may indicate that somebody does not want to hear what you are saying.

"Speak No Evil"

If somebody does not like what you are saying, they will often cover up their mouth. Ask a young child if they are lying and immediately, they will cover up their mouth with their hands. We become more subtle with this as adults. People's hands will often be drawn to their mouths either when they are speaking or when hearing something that they don't like.

Other signs of discomfort associated with the mouth are the biting of the lower lip and the narrowing of the lips. You may have heard the expression "I really had to bite my tongue." This can also be seen in the biting of the lower lip.

Another sign of discomfort is scratching at the neck or pulling on the collar. The phrase "they are a real pain in the neck," can be taken literally.

Body language should not be identified in isolation, but in clusters. A baseline of normal body language behaviour must be established first. For example, if somebody has a habit of scratching their neck, it doesn't necessarily mean that they are displaying signs of discomfort. They may just have an itchy neck. However, if they are displaying signs of discomfort, other nonverbal signals will also be displayed. Imagine somebody that has had a stressful day. When they arrive home, they may say, "At last I can finally relax!" Their body language opens up and visible relaxation occurs in their face and body.

Making a Decision

Another useful body language pattern to be aware of is the stroking of the chin. Men tend to stroke the chin between the thumb and the forefinger, pulling down on the chin whereas women tend to have their knuckles pointing upwards and pull away from the chin.

Non Verbal Clues

Chin stroking often involves looking up or looking down, or a defocussing of the eyes, as access to the internal decision making process takes place. This can also be accompanied by a narrowing of the eyes. If a man has a beard, he will often stroke his beard around the chin area as a comforter rather than when solely evaluating. For a more advanced understanding of body Language the reader is referred to "HOW TO READ ANY BODY" by the author.

CHAPTER 16

Closing The Sale

"You can have everything in life you want if you will just help enough other people get what they want."

Zig Ziglar

The close is just asking for the order and is as simple as saying to the customer, "Are we going to do this?" or, "What do you think?" Many salespeople don't like asking for the order because, at this point, it is clear whether the customer is going to proceed or not and people don't like to fail.

ABC

Early in my sales career, I came across the acronym ABC, which stands for "always be closing." On hearing about this for the first time, I thought that it sounded a little gimmicky. A far better way to think of this *is* "always be clarifying."

When conducting the fact find, gaining information and presenting the solution, clarification should be ongoing to minimise the likelihood of any surprises at the end. The best way to close is to "always be clarifying." This means checking the customer's thoughts when moving through the sales process.

CLOSING IN

Some Closes

A classic close is the "sharp-angled" close. For example, if a customer asks if something comes in a particular colour, let's say blue, the salesperson would then say.

"If it came in blue, would you buy it?"

This is not very subtle and a far better question is to relate the choice of colour to the list of criteria. For example,

"How important is the blue colour when selecting....."

There is a close called the assumptive close. This presupposes that someone is going to buy. Rather than describing this as a close, I prefer to refer to this as a language pattern. This can be used throughout the sales process. It works on the assumption that the person is going to buy the product. An example is,

"When you use this system, you will find that......"

We are not going to cover all the classic closes because if the groundwork hasn't been carried out properly, it is irrelevant what close has been used, it simply won't work.

An exception to this is the "puppy dog close" and it makes good business sense. With the puppy dog close, the owner of the puppy allows you to take the puppy home, knowing that you will love it so much that you won't want to give it back. The puppy dog close has the effect of de-risking and transferring the risk from the buyer to the seller. An example would be:

> *"I am so convinced that you are going to love this piece of software. Why don't you try it for free for a month and let me know what you think? If you don't like it, then simply pay nothing."*

"Shut Up!"

Many people find themselves in sales because they like to talk. Talking too much is a major weakness when it comes to closing. The biggest mistake is asking for the order and then failing to remain silent. There is a tendency amongst some salespeople to start answering the question that they have just asked. For example:

> *"What do you think? Shall we just proceed with the paperwork?"*

Even before the customer has had a chance to answer the question, many salespeople start talking.

> *"Well, if it's too expensive, we can always reduce the cost a bit"* or *"If you feel that you would like to think about it, that's fine."*

The Golden Rule

The one who speaks first loses. The golden rule is to ask for the order and then simply "shut up." Remain quiet and do not speak until the customer says something. This can sometimes take a while and can feel like an eternity, but the customer must be allowed a chance to speak and think. Whatever you do, if the customer is displaying some chin stroking, do not speak until they speak first!

OBJECTION HANDLING

If the groundwork has been done properly, the number of objections will be lower. When "always be clarifying", a lot of the objections will be answered during your discussion.

If somebody says, "Well, this is great but we're not looking to replace this just yet", you have not asked the right questions. This has been a failure to establish criteria early on. Objections can be seen as questions where people are looking for more information. Sometimes customers, as part of the game, like to keep a few objections back.

The Smokescreen

Very often, there is a smokescreen because people just don't want to give the real objection. This can be because the objection is personal, they don't want confrontation, or they don't want to appear rude. They may like their current supplier and have a good relationship with them. They may also be aware that the real objection could be handled if it was revealed. A way around this is to say,

"Apart from this, is there anything else?"

With this phrase, the aim is to uncover the real objection.

"If we can get this fixed, would you be willing to go ahead?"

Feel Felt Found

This is a very effective method for handling objections. First of all, we pace the customer's or client's expectations.

> *"It's perfectly natural to be apprehensive about changing supplier and I understand how you **feel**. In fact, many of the businesses that I have spoken to **felt** the same way. However, when they switched to us, they **found** that they made significant cost savings and that their client approval ratings rose by up to forty three per cent."*

It's Hard to Displace an Old Friend

When I first entered the field of intermediary sales, I was working for a life insurance company selling life insurance and investment products to financial advisers. The company that I was working for was one of many companies looking to get a share of the products recommended by the financial adviser which they would then recommend to their clients. At the time, one of the more experienced salespeople told me that there is a pecking order. The financial adviser will have a good business and personal relationship with the representative from one company. That individual would get the lion's share of the business. When this representative left a company, the number two choice would get a larger share and so on. Any attempt to point out the flaws in the chosen company would be met with resistance.

Think about two close friends. It is difficult to break that friendship. They will have spent a lot of time together, have common interests and will support each other. People often have their closest friends but will have other friends for activities or interests that their best friend does not engage in.

In a business context, when dealing with intermediary sales, be aware that this can be an issue and it is better to explore a niche solution where the preferred competitor is not operating. It is better to aim for a smaller slice first, rather than going in all guns blazing to begin with. Getting some business is better than getting no business at all.

You Know What They Are So Prepare

Good salespeople prepare. They know what the objections are, who the competitors are, and how to reframe objections. Ideally, planning to pre handle as many objections as possible should be considered, particularly the top five objections. The vast majority of objections will be similar. When hearing one, it is important to listen carefully and never to interrupt the customer while they are speaking.

Many salespeople feel the need to jump right in when hearing an objection and start putting the customer right. Remember, we want to be in uptime listening to the customer and not internalising images. It is a good idea, when the customer has finished speaking, to summarise the customer's objection and repeat it back to them. Let's just suppose that it was a price issue.

> *"Just to check my understanding, from what you are saying, that the price is the only issue and you're happy with the other parts of the product. Is that correct?"*

In this example, the objection has been repeated back to them and a closed question is used to narrow this down. The customer has accepted that they want the product or service and it is just a question of price and terms.

We are now entering the area of negotiation, and this will be covered in the next section.

NEGOTIATION

Negotiation forms part of the sales process. When selling something, not only should the sales pitch be planned but also the negotiation, together with the bargaining power and trade-offs.

Establishing a Win/Win

It is essential to establish a win/win. The customer wants to feel that they will win and the salesperson also wants to win. Negotiation is a game, and in some cultures, it is expected, and is a very important part of the sales process.

Negotiation can be regarded as part of the closing process. When entering the negotiation phase, the customer has already decided to go ahead, as long as some additional criteria will be met. The principle to go ahead has been established.

Many people feel uncomfortable negotiating and are terrible negotiators. Negotiating is bargaining and can be regarded as tailor making the solution to the customer's needs. Off the peg solutions do not always fit. When negotiating, a sharpened awareness is required, together with a robust questioning process. The customer is aware of the benefits of the product or service and the use of questioning clarifies their specific requirements. Questioning also uncovers and highlights any weaknesses in the customer's position. It is also worth remembering that when entering the negotiation stage, both parties have decided to go ahead. If the deal does not go ahead, both parties now will suffer a loss.

Let's imagine that price is an obstacle. The customer's strength is that they know that you want the order and that you may move on price. The salesperson's strength is that they know that the customer is now convinced of the need and will be disadvantaged if the deal does not go ahead. Simply pointing out or asking them what would happen if they did not take action is powerful.

If, for example, it was IT security, you could ask them of the implications if they did not adopt your solution. What would it mean for their business and reputation if their system was hacked and this allowed personal details to be revealed?

Narrowing It Down

We now need to establish exactly what the customer wants. For example,

> "What exactly are you looking for, to enable you to proceed today?"

At this point, the customer is going to say exactly what they're looking for. They then need to be pinned down. The statement needs to be repeated back, stating exactly what they are looking for and a closed question used to clarify this.

> "I just want to make sure that I understand correctly. If we do this for you, then you will go ahead, is that correct?"

If the customer then says,

> "I want to think about it."

Simply ask them,

> "What is it that you need to think about to enable you to proceed today?"

Buyer's Remorse

Buyer's remorse occurs when somebody purchases something and then either regrets the purchase or thinks that they could have got a much better deal. Think about a purchase that you made where you asked for a discount. You may even have been offered a discount without asking. Many people have never been involved in a negotiation situation and if that's the case, just pretend for this example.

Imagine asking for a discount and the seller immediately gives a ten per cent discount. Receiving a discount may feel good at the time. However, as time passes by, a niggling thought often emerges. If the seller was willing to give ten per cent immediately, how much more could they have given?"

Now imagine asking for a discount where you really had to work hard to get any. You were initially offered nothing but eventually managed to get ten per cent. Remember, when a discount is first given, this is only an offer which you can accept or reject. A good negotiator will make you work hard for any discount and often compliment you on your negotiation skills. They often finish it up with a statement such as,

> *"You drive a hard bargain and I don't normally give a discount."*

In both examples, the final discount was still the same ten per cent. In the first situation, it may have felt that more could have been given and in the second, when receiving a discount from an experienced negotiator, it may have felt that you were lucky to have got anything at all. Yet it is the same level of discount.

We have to be aware of this. Any deal must be a win/win arrangement to make sure that each party gets what they want and are happy with the arrangement. A good negotiation strategy is to make sure that customers work for a discount. Then compliment the customer on their negotiating skills at the end.

Anything that comes too easy, is often not appreciated nor valued. We have to be very careful when we're negotiating and not give away anything too easily and needlessly.

The Good Guy, Bad Guy Approach

This is a very useful approach, but be aware that control is lost when using this. In many sales situations, good rapport can be built with a client and a presentation delivered well. Then it comes to that moment of asking for the order and there is an objection. Suddenly, instead of being on the same side as the customer, we find ourselves on the opposing side.

The "good guy, bad guy" is a useful approach to use in this instance. Instead of saying "no", a third party is relied upon to say "no". This is commonplace in car sales. The approach is very simple. An example is,

> "I would love to give you a discount and if it was my company, I would do so immediately. The problem is that the owner of the business is quite a tricky individual and he doesn't give discounts. Let me speak to him. Aside from price, are there any other reasons that we cannot proceed today?"

With car sales, the salesperson will go to see the sales manager. The sales manager then prepares a deal for the salesperson to take back to the customer. Double glazing salespeople use this technique and will often be seen to make a phone call when in our house.

When people ask for something additional to that agreed upon, a useful phrase is,

> "Yes, we can do that and the price for it is..."

If the price is an issue, simply clarify what they are looking to invest (not pay).

> "I sense we are close to an agreement. What is it that you need to go ahead today?"

Never give away any discount without knowing exactly what you have to give away. Prepare for the salami, where customers keep asking for more and more. The way to handle this is to say, "Yes, that's fine and the cost for this is."

HOW TO NEGOTIATE PRICE

The cost or price is going to come up at virtually every meeting, and it is important to be prepared. The first thing to do is to frame the price and in doing so, it is necessary to understand price anchoring.

Price Anchoring

People make decisions by using relative distances from two anchor points. This is an incredibly powerful technique. It takes advantage of one of the hard-wired biases within us. Notice how two statements feel different.

> "The cost to hire this room is $5000."
>
> "The cost to hire this room can be anything up to $10,000 but you can hire it for $5000."

Let's assume that both statements are true. Notice how in the first statement the cost is stated which may be acceptable or expensive depending on your viewpoint. There is no context to measure against in the first statement, whereas in the second it appears like you are getting a bargain. It is important to be honest with customers. In this example, room hire rates vary and the $10,000 price may apply for a wedding.

Remember the Wingtips.

Now that we understand price anchoring when somebody first lays out their position, if they're good at negotiating, it will always be an exaggerated position. They know that this forms part of anchoring. In negotiations, people often start with extremes of positions at the wingtips and move to the centre or fuselage.

A Sharp Intake of Breath

A classic technique in negotiation that works well is known as "the flinch." It doesn't matter what price is quoted, just breathe in and flinch. This is often accompanied by a slight frowning as if the price is very expensive.

I first came across the flinch years ago whilst driving to work from my home in Edinburgh to Glasgow in Scotland. After listening to various radio stations and exhausting my music collection, I decided to use the time productively to learn new skills. Being in charge of the training budget, I decided to buy some audio training to learn negotiation skills.

While listening to the recordings, the author described the flinch. On hearing it, I thought that I couldn't possibly do this. Even the thought of it made me cringe and I was not convinced that it was going to work. At that time, I had a powerboat and was looking for accessories for it. I thought that I would try the newly learnt technique. Upon entering the chandlers, I asked the seller the price of the accessories. As soon as the price was stated, I immediately flinched. The person serving me was not aware of the flinch and started offering way more discount than was necessary. It had worked! I did the same when buying some audio equipment and it worked too.

After flinching, it is important to be quiet. Allow the other person to do the talking. Many people are poor negotiators and start throwing away needless discounts straight away. If someone does the flinch to you, be aware of this.

The Power of the Walk Away

A big mistake when buying something is to appear too keen. It is important to give the impression that you are not desperate for the order. Experienced negotiators know this and are willing to walk away. This is often a ploy. Knowing and determining the walk away point, the point at which the deal becomes unviable, is essential. Know this and stick to it.

Time to Get Creative

Price is likely to be an issue when negotiating. Sometimes, the price cannot be changed, but the offer can be made more attractive. Let's suppose at this stage that the price is the main obstacle. It's time to think creatively. Let's suppose that it is an IT system that you are selling. Is there anything that can be included that is low cost to your firm but has high perceived value? Perhaps training could be included, where people in the firm could be trained on how to get the best out of the IT system? This is a clever strategy, as it enables more rapport with the client to be built from spending more time with them.

Perhaps the business is short of space and they need meeting rooms to hold seminars for their clients. Is there a space that could be offered for use? Another option is to offer access to experts in your company that could help contribute to a newsletter or speak at events.

Think creatively, the more your profit margins can be protected using high perceived value benefits, then the better this will be for your bottom line.

The Upchunk

I call this technique "the upchunk", and many political interviewers use it. Interviewers often try to trap the interviewees, and lawyers use this technique in court. In short, you get someone to agree to something and then link that to something else. An example makes it clearer.

> "Do you believe that it is important that people should be able to walk around safely in this neighbourhood?"
> "Yes."
> "Could you explain to me why you have failed to do anything about the rising number of attacks on people in this neighbourhood?"

Be very aware if this is being done to you. The upchunk can be used to help reframe the picture when negotiating.

Let's consider recommending life insurance. The client has accepted the need for life assurance, but the cost is an issue. Let's look at how the upchunk can be used. First, a more generalised context is needed, followed by a more specific question which relates to the first one.

> ***Example 1***
> "Do you think that it is important to make sure that your family is financially secure, if anything were ever to happen to you? "
> "Yes"
> "Is $100 per month too much to pay to provide for your family's security, if anything were to happen to you?"

Let's look at investing for school fees.

Example 2

"Do you think that it is important to provide the best education possible for your children?"

"Of course!"

"Do you think investing £200 per month for the benefit of your children's education to give them the best start in life is worthwhile?"

The upchunk is very powerful and works very well when used in front of other people. People use it all the time in everyday life without being aware of it.

You won't always get what you want when negotiating every time. Remember, don't look too pleased with yourself if you do.

Anyone for a Nibble?

The nibble occurs once the deal has been struck, the price has been agreed and the customer has committed to buying. Once you have agreed on the price, the customer may then come back and say,

"This does include free delivery, doesn't it?"

At this point, there is a tendency to give in and confirm that it does because we don't want to lose the sale. An example of this would be when buying a car and the price has been agreed. The customer then asks,

"This does include mud flaps, doesn't it?"

At this point, stand firm and say authoritatively,

> *"Of course, we would be delighted to fit mud flaps and the price for this is….."*

Another version of the nibble is "the quivering pen." The customer has a pen in their hand and is just about to sign the contract. The customer then looks up at you and asks if free delivery is included? The reply is the same.

Things to Be Aware of

When negotiating a price, specific numbers have more of an impact than rounded numbers. Something priced at $197.98 sounds more convincing than something priced at $200. If something is priced precisely, it is more believable.

Beware of the higher authority tactic. If somebody says they have to refer to a higher authority to get a decision, which could be their boss, then simply say,

> "Great, when can you arrange for me to meet him/her?"

CHAPTER 17

Post Sales Meeting

"If you are not taking care of your customer,

your competitor will."

Bob Hooey

There are different types of after sales service depending upon the sales process. It may be that a sale takes place over several meetings. Closing may not be possible after one meeting. However, in other cases, we get a sale after one meeting.

POST SALE BLUES

As we move into the after sales process, we move away from the initial excitement of the sale, getting the order and into the routine part of followup and service. For many, this is the least exciting part of the job, but is an important part.

During a meeting, if promises are made or follow up information is required, these must be actioned. Often people promise to do something and just don't do it. When I started in sales, somebody said to me if you want to be successful, "do what you say you're going to do, do it properly, and do it on time."

I remember meeting with a sales representative from a company and asked about their products and services. I was genuinely interested and the sales representative promised to send the information to me. The presentation had taken place and all that was required was an email with the information. Yet this never took place. This is incredibly easy to do and yet so many fail to do this.

If you promise to do something, do what you say that you are going to do, do it on time and do it properly, then you will be surprised by how well this is received by your customers or clients and you will stand out.

PLEASE FIND ATTACHED.....

If the sale has not been closed or this is a multistage sale, the customer may at this point ask for more information. In some cases, this is a fob off. However, in other cases, it can be a genuine interest, particularly if a further evaluation has to take place.

One of my pet hates, when asking for more information, is receiving an email saying, "please find attached", which contains a complicated forty page pdf document. Think about this for a moment. Imagine that you have a hobby that you are passionate about. An email relating to your hobby then arrives and contains a forty page pdf document. Would you read all of it, particularly if it is heavy going? If you are like most people, you wouldn't read all of it. If that's the case for information that we are interested in, what chance is there of somebody reading a complicated forty page pdf document? Some people would read it, but the vast majority just won't. There's more to it than that. Simply sending out a forty page pdf document gives the impression of not putting in any effort and just wanting to send out an attachment.

How then can we stand out from other companies and other salespeople? Remember that the confused mind always says no and the suspicious mind always says no. Summarising the key points in the document in a few sentences, together with referencing the relevant page numbers, makes it much easier for the customer to understand. This communicates to the customer that an effort has been made to make it easy for them. Doing this will make you stand out from your competitors because so few people will put the effort in. Some industries are heavily regulated and some care is needed when sending information out. Check with your industry first. There is usually a way to summarise what is in the document and make reference to it.

A sales trainer, years ago, mentioned that we should always go the extra mile or kilometre. I don't think that you have to go the extra mile or kilometre, simply going an extra few yards, or an extra few metres will usually make enough of a difference to stand out.

POST SALES SERVICE

After the sale, the temptation is to move on to the next customer. The customer that has just bought the product or service can often be forgotten about. This is a classic mistake because a customer, that has just bought our product or service, may be in buyer's remorse. They are looking for reassurance. We need to make sure that we reassure them that they have made the right decision.

Think about making a large purchase. It is at this point that you are at your most vulnerable and are looking for reassurance. If somebody says "Why did you buy that?" inferring that it was a bad decision, a defence of the purchase begins. If more people ask this question, then doubt starts to creep in. Now compare this to when someone asks you as to why you bought something that you bought years ago. In this case, you will not be so concerned because you are happy with the purchase and don't need any external validation.

Somebody who has bought your product or service can be a fantastic source of referrals. Providing excellent post sale service gains extra credibility and referrals. On completion of the sale, we should explain what will happen next, who will be in touch and what will be required. A good habit to get into is to make a telephone call after the sale to check that the customer is satisfied with the progress. This is useful, as not everyone in an organisation is as efficient as they could be.

Some people feel uncomfortable contacting customers after the sale, just in case there has been a problem. If a problem has occurred, this provides an opportunity to engage and fix it. Solving a problem can cause even greater customer loyalty. Things do go wrong. It is how we react and fix it that creates the correct impression.

REFERRALS

Existing customers can represent a fantastic referral base. People like to tell stories, particularly if they are satisfied. Many salespeople ask for referrals by asking,

> *"Do you know of anyone who would benefit from the product or service?"*

The answer from the customer is usually,

> *"No, but if I think of anyone, I will recommend them to you."*

A better way to ask is,

> *"What firms do you know that would benefit from this?"*

They may then mention the name of a firm, to which you reply,

> *"Do you have a contact name there?"*

If they give you a contact name, ask,

> *"Would it be alright if I mentioned that you said to give them a call?"*

Try the Clairvoyant's Trick

The clairvoyant's trick is to lead people to select somebody that may be suitable for a referral. When asking for a referral, it's much better to frame the situation first and then ask for the request, which then leads to an answer.

"We grow our business through referrals and it would be fantastic if you could help us with our growth. Who can you think of that would benefit from our service?"

Wait for the reply and if nothing comes, prompt them, just as a clairvoyant would.

"Perhaps it could be somebody that you work with, or someone in your immediate family, or somebody that you know down at the Golf Club."

Using this prompting technique can help steer people to identify those that would be suitable. Generally, people are pleased to give referrals if they are happy with the product or service. If they say no, that's fine because if you don't ask, then you don't get.

CHAPTER 18

Conclusion

"To succeed, jump as quickly at opportunities
as you do at conclusions."

Benjamin Franklin

Many people like a structured approach and methods that will work in whatever type of sales environment that they are in. This gives a framework and acts a bit like a train track. The principles have been covered in detail however, sometimes the train can get derailed. In this situation, communication skills are required to get us back on track.

Human communication is complicated. Much of this is going on outside of our awareness but is still being processed unconsciously. We are only aware of a small proportion of what is going on. Working on BSRA (Belief, State Control, Rapport Building and Awareness) skills is at the core of success.

Belief sets out the foundations of what we believe to be possible and true. In this book, numerous examples have been cited of seemingly impossible occurrences, which have been well documented. Belief is both empowering and limiting. If it can be believed, then it can be conceived. Argue for your weakness, and it is yours.

The ability to control your state and recall previous resources will dictate your success, not just with sales, but in all your communication situations. The ability to control state was demonstrated, when a previously thought of as impossible amount of weight was lifted, by Eddie Hall. There are methods for controlling your state and following the methods shown will enable this to be done. It is a skill that requires practice and then can be done easily and effectively.

Rapport building skills form the very bedrock of communication. With rapport, just about anything is possible and without it, very little. The degree to which you can build rapport with another will govern your success in all areas of your life. Rapport is something that can be learnt and the methods practised until it becomes incorporated into your everyday life. The more alike that you are to the other person then the more rapport that you will build with them. The more that interest can be moved from self interest, to an interest in the other person then the more profound this change will be.

The final piece in the jigsaw is learning to develop a sharpened awareness. The more the transfer is away from an inward focus to an external focus, then the greater will be the effect. This is something that can be developed by paying attention to watching how people walk, talk, the words that they use and how they communicate. Simply noticing their body language, facial expressions and how they react to situations is key.

It has been said that a book should not be judged by its cover, but sometimes we don't have time to read the story, and the cover is the only clue that we have as to the contents of the book.

Practice the methods and notice how much more interesting and fun life can be. Have fun and enjoy your new skill set.

Thank you for reading this book.

If you enjoyed this book, it would help enormously if you would be kind enough to leave a review because of the way the algorithms work and really does help authors. Many thanks **Leave a review here** https://linktr.ee/DerekBorthwick

Coaching, training and speaking enquiries, info@power2mind.com

Get Your Complimentary Rapid Learning Accelerator Audio & Bonus Chapter "The Hot Button" at https://www.themindofsales.com

See over for other titles available.

208

References

Bandler, R. (1976). *The structure of magic*. Palo Alto, CA: Science and Behavior Books.

Bandler, R., Grinder, J., & Andreas, S. (1990). *Frogs into princes: Neuro Linguistic Programming*. London: Eden Grove.

Bandler, R., Grinder, J., & Andreas, S. (1994). *Reframing: neuro-linguistic programming and the transformation of meaning*. Moab Utah: Real People Press.

Bandler, R., Grinder, J., & DeLozier, J. (1996). *Patterns of the hypnotic techniques of Milton H. Erickson, M.D.* Scotts Valley, CA: Grinder & Associates.

Bandler, R. (2008). *Richard Bandlers guide to trance-formation*. Deerfield Beach, FL: Health Communications, Inc.

Birdwhistell, R. L. (1971). *Kinesics and context: Essays on body-motion communication*. London.

Bolstad, R. (2011). *Resolve: a new model of therapy*. Carmarthen, Wales: Crown House Pub.

Brown, D. (2007). *Tricks of the mind*. London: Channel 4 Books.

Bruce Lipton https://www.brucelipton.com/category/topics/new-biology

Childre, D. L., Atkinson, M., McCraty, R., & Tomasino, D. (2001). *Science of the heart: exploring the role of the heart*. Boulder Creek, CA: HeartMath Research Center, Institute of HearMath.

Cialdini, R. B. (2007). *Influence: the psychology of persuasion: Robert B. Cialdini*. New York: Collins.

Cialdini, R. B. (2018). *Pre-suasion: a revolutionary way to influence and persuade*. New York: Simon & Schuster Paperbacks.

Clark, B. C., Mahato, N. K., Nakazawa, M., Law, T. D., & Thomas, J. S. (2014). The power of the mind: the cortex as a critical determinant of muscle strength/weakness. *Journal of Neurophysiology*, *112*(12), 3219–3226. doi: 10.1152/jn.00386.2014

Clark, L. V. (1960). Effect of Mental Practice on the Development of a Certain Motor Skill. *Research Quarterly. American Association for Health, Physical Education and Recreation*, *31*(4), 560–569. doi: 10.1080/10671188.1960.10613109

Covey, S. R. (2016). *The 7 habits of highly effective people*. San Francisco, CA: FranklinCovey Co.

Cuddy, A. J. C., Schultz, S. J., & Fosse, N. E. (2018). P-Curving a More Comprehensive Body of Research on Postural Feedback Reveals Clear Evidential

Value for Power-Posing Effects: Reply to Simmons and Simonsohn (2017). *Psychological Science*, *29*(4), 656–666. doi: 10.1177/0956797617746749

Dantalion, J. (2008). *Mind Control Language Patterns*. Lieu de publication inconnu: Mind Control Publishing.

Dawson, R. (2014, October 14). The Secrets of Power Negotiating. Retrieved from https://www.audible.com/pd/The-Secrets-of-Power-Negotiating-Audiobook/B00NMQVS9G

Eagleman, D. (2012). *Incognito*. Rearsby: Clipper Large Print.

Elman, D. (1970). *Hypnotherapy*. Glendale, CA: Westwood Pub. Co.

Estabrooks, G. H. (1968). *Hypnotism*. New York: Dutton.

Grinder, J., & Bandler, R. (1985). *Trance-formations: neuro-linguistic programming and the structure of hypnosis*. Moab: Real People Press.

Hall, E. (2018). *Strongman: my story*. London: Virgin Books.

Heller, S., & Steele, T. L. (2009). *Monsters & magical sticks: theres no such thing as hypnosis?* Tempe, AZ: Original Falcon Press.

Cedar Books. (1988). *How to win friends and influence people*. London.

Hull, C. L. (1968). *Hypnosis and suggestibility An experimental approach*. New York: Appleton-Century-Crofts.

Jung, C. (2016). Psychological Types. doi: 10.4324/9781315512334

Kimbro, D. P., Hill, N., & Hill, N. (1997). *Think and grow rich: a Black choice*. New York: Fawcett Columbine.

Klaff, O. (2011). *Pitch anything: an innovative method for presenting, persuading and winning the deal*. New York, NY: McGraw-Hill.

Klopfer, B. (1957). Psychological Variables In Human Cancer. *Journal of Projective Techniques*, *21*(4), 331–340. doi: 10.1080/08853126.1957.10380794

Knox, R. (2014, January 10). Half Of A Drug's Power Comes From Thinking It Will Work. Retrieved June 16, 2020, from https://www.npr.org/sections/health-shots/2014/01/10/261406721/half-a-drugs-power-comes-from-thinking-it-will-work

Koch, R. (1998). *80/20 Principle: the secret of achieving more with less. (Alternate title: Eighty-twenty principle)*. New York: Currency.

Kolenda, N. (2013). *Methods of persuasion: how to use psychology to influence human behavior*. Place of publication not identified: publisher not identified.

Ledochowski, I. (2003). *The deep trance training manual*. Carmarthen, Wales: Crown House Pub.

Lorayne, H. (1979). *How to develop a super-power memory*. Wellingborough: A. Thomas.

Macknik, S. L., Martinez-Conde, S., & Blakeslee, S. (2012). *Sleights of mind: what the neuroscience of magic reveals about our brains*. London: Profile.

Maclean, P. D. (1988). Triune Brain. *Comparative Neuroscience and Neurobiology*, 126–128. doi: 10.1007/978-1-4899-6776-3_51

Mason, A. A. (1952). Case of Congenital Ichthyosiform Erythrodermia of Brocq treated by Hypnosis. *Bmj*, *2*(4781), 422–423. doi: 10.1136/bmj.2.4781.422

McGill, O. (1947). *The encyclopedia of genuine stage hypnotism*. Colon, MI: Abbotts Magic Novelty Co.

Michael H., M. I., C., G., & Volker. (2014, September 29). Neurobiological foundations of neurologic music therapy: rhythmic entrainment and the motor system. Retrieved from https://www.frontiersin.org/articles/10.3389/fpsyg.2014.01185/full

Miller, G. A. (1956). The magical number seven, plus or minus two: some limits on our capacity for processing information. *Psychological Review*, *63*(2), 81–97. doi: 10.1037/h0043158

Murphy, J. (2013). *The power of your subconscious mind, Dr. Joseph Murphy*. Place of publication not identified: Wildside Press.

Navarro, J., & Karlins, M. (2015). *What every Body is saying: an ex-Fbi agents guide to speed-reading people*. New York, NY: Harper Collins.

OBrien, D. (1994). *How to develop a perfect memory*. London: Headline.

Pascual-Leone, A., Nguyet, D., Cohen, L. G., Brasil-Neto, J. P., Cammarota, A., & Hallett, M. (1995). Modulation of muscle responses evoked by transcranial magnetic stimulation during the acquisition of new fine motor skills. *Journal of Neurophysiology*, *74*(3), 1037–1045. doi: 10.1152/jn.1995.74.3.1037

Pease, A. (1997). *How to read others thoughts by their gestures*. London: Sheldon.

Pulos, L. (2014, October 14). The Biology of Empowerment. Retrieved from https://www.audible.com/pd/The-Biology-of-Empowerment-Audiobook/B00O3I9V8M

Rossi, E. L. (1993). *The psychobiology of mind-body healing: new concepts of therapeutic hypnosis*. New York: Norton.

NLP power Dr. David Snyder. Retrieved from https://www.youtube.com/user/SanDiegoKarate

NLP power https://www.nlppower.com/product/killer-influence/

Schwarz, B. E. (1960). Ordeal by serpents, fire and strychnine. *Psychiatric Quarterly*, *34*(3), 405–429. doi: 10.1007/bf01562423

Syed, M. (2010). *How champions are made*. London: Fourth Estate.

Talbot, M. (1991). *The holographic universe*. London: Grafton Books.

Trial of arthroscopic evaluation of osteoarthritis of the knee by image processing. (1991). *Arthroscopy: The Journal of Arthroscopic & Related Surgery*, *7*(4), 398–399. doi: 10.1016/0749-8063(91)90020-x

Tversky, A., & Kahneman, D. (1974). Judgment under Uncertainty: Heuristics and Biases. *Science, 185*(4157), 1124–1131. doi: 10.1126/science.185.4157.1124

Watson, J. B. (1913). Psychology as the behaviorist views it. *Psychological Review, 20*(2), 158–177. doi: 10.1037/h0074428

Welch, C. (2015). *How the art of medicine makes the science more effective: becoming the medicine we practice*. London: Singing Dragon.

Printed in Great Britain
by Amazon